Research Skills Series

Real World Research Skills

An Introduction to Factual, International, Judicial, Legislative, and Regulatory Research

Second Edition

By Peggy Garvin

TheCapitol.Net

TheCapitol.Net, Inc. is a non-partisan firm that annually provides continuing professional education and information for thousands of government and business leaders that strengthens representative government and the rule of law.

Our publications and courses, written and taught by *current* Washington insiders who are all independent subject matter experts, show how Washington works.™ Our products and services can be found on our web site at *<www.TheCapitol.Net>*.

Additional copies of *Real World Research Skills* can be ordered online: *<www.RealWorldResearchSkills.com>*.

Citation Form—URLs: We use a standard style for all web addresses, also known as Uniform Resource Locators (URLs). URLs appear in text next to the first mention of the resource being described, and are surrounded with open and close angle brackets.

For URLs that have the standard web addressing form at the beginning of the URL of "http://www." we show only the initial "www." For example, the URL "http://www.domainname.com" will appear in text and tables as "*<www.domainname.com>*".

For URLs that begin with anything other than "www.", such as "http://thomas.loc.gov", the URL will appear in text and tables as "*<http://thomas.loc.gov>*". For example, the URL "http://www3.domain.gov" will appear in text and tables as "*<http://www3.domain.gov>*".

Design and production by Zaccarine Design, Inc., Evanston, IL; 847-864-3994.

Summary Table of Contents

About the Author

Peggy Garvin is an independent information consultant. Her company, Garvin Information Consulting, provides training, writing, and consulting to help professionals make the best use of the wealth of U.S. government information online. Peggy has worked with government information, libraries, and information technology over her twenty-year-plus career with the Library of Congress Congressional Research Service and in the private sector. She earned her Master of Library Science degree from Syracuse University.

Peggy contributes to TheCapitol.Net's *Congressional Deskbook* and edits the annual reference book *e-Government and Web Directory: U.S. Federal Government Online* (Lanham, MD: Bernan Press). Her column, "The Government Domain," appears in the law and technology webzine, LLRX.com. She also writes a government information column for the magazine *Searcher* (Medford, NJ: Information Today, Inc.).

Table of Contents

Chapter 4 Judicial Branch Research 49

Chapter 5 Executive Branch Research 57

Introduction

"Knowledge is of two kinds: we know a subject ourselves, or we know where we can find information upon it."

—Samuel Johnson (1709-1784), as quoted in the *Life of Samuel Johnson* by James Boswell

Even in the 18th century, scholars realized it was not possible to know everything worth knowing; sometimes, we have to look it up. Fortunately for Dr. Johnson, he did not have to be familiar with so many sources and so many different techniques for finding information. He did, however, recognize the value of knowing where to find information. What today's Internet-enabled workers have discovered is that we also need to know *how to search* and *how to evaluate* what we find.

This book compiles basic advice, techniques, reference information, and resources to help working professionals find accurate information quickly. It is written particularly for those whose work involves tapping into federal government information. The book began as a set of materials for TheCapitol.Net's seminar, "Research Tools and Techniques: Refining Your Online and Offline Searches." It is designed to be used as a complement to that seminar or independently as a desk reference.

The first and second chapters cover practical principles of research and online searching, including the general search engines. These sections include checklists and advice that are applicable to many different research tasks and many different databases and search engines.

The third, fourth, and fifth chapters present resources for federal legislative, judicial, and executive branch research.

The sixth chapter covers starting points for state and international research on the web.

The final chapter, "Experts and Insiders," has tips for tapping into that vital Washington information resource: people.

In our knowledge economy, more and more people—with a wide range of education and experience—are moving into jobs that require some information-gathering skills. The research training provided at many schools lays a foundation, but often does not prepare us for the varied demands of the working world. This book is not intended to cover academic research resources, nor is it a comprehensive listing of Washington research resources. It supplies advice based on working knowledge and experience, and pointers to good places to start one's search.

We hope it will be useful to you. If you have suggestions for additions or changes to the book, please contact us: Publisher, TheCapitol.Net, PO Box 25706, Alexandria, VA 22313-5706, fax: 202-466-5370, email: deskbook@thecapitol.net.

Introducing the Research Skills Series

We have provided icons to alert you to important points.

Search Guide

gives you answers on the search process.

Research Tips

are practical hints to make your search easier.

Information Resources

are places for you to look for specific answers to your questions.

Checklist

is a quick list of ways to improve your searching.

Reference Information

describes and defines basic information.

RealWorldResearchSkills.com

Chapter One

Before You Start Your Research

Research involves more than typing words into a search box. Knowing how to prepare before researching and how to keep yourself on course during a research project are critical skills that can give you a competitive advantage.

This chapter provides checklists to help you develop an effective approach to real world research.

§1.0 Plan Your Research

A research project, small or large, begins with either an assignment from someone else or with your own recognition that you need more information. Either way, you can make your research more efficient and effective by assessing both the information need and the available information sources before you dive into a search engine or pick up the phone to make that first call.

Research consumes time and money, resources you do not want to waste. Planning can make your search more efficient and lead to better results. Your planning may consist of taking a few seconds to think before looking up a quick fact, or it may involve developing a structured strategy for a complex research project—and adjusting that strategy as needed. Whatever the size of the project, there are four steps to consider:

§1.1 Identify the Precise Question You Are Trying to Answer

How will the answer be relevant to the problem you are trying to solve?

- **Do you understand the question?** Research tasks, big and small, often go awry because the question to be answered is misleading or vague. This can happen when people build assumptions into their question. For example, someone may ask you to find the transcript of a recent congressional hearing on the THOMAS legislative web site, assuming incorrectly that THOMAS has these transcripts. Someone may ask for the federal poverty level figure, assuming there is one number. In fact there are two federal government measures of poverty, one for statistical purposes and one for determining eligibility for certain federal programs, and these figures may vary depending on location or family size. (See Institute for Research on Poverty FAQ, <*www.irp.wisc.edu/faqs/faq1.htm*>.) Poorly worded questions are common because it is difficult to ask for information that you do not know. For example, someone may ask you to find "everything" on a topic simply because they do not know enough about the topic to fine-tune their request.

  How do you handle a poorly worded or poorly informed question? If you are researching an issue for someone else, the most important question to ask the requestor is, "How will you be using this information?" Understanding why the question is being asked and how it will be used will help you select relevant sources and produce usable research results. For example, your boss may ask for information on ice-skating in Pennsylvania. The type of information you seek will vary, depending on whether the information is needed for a decision to buy an ice-skating rink, to prepare for a meeting with ice-skating advocates, to cite statistics about the economic benefits of ice-skating rinks, or to plan a family vacation.

- **Questions to ask:**
    - How will you be using this information?
    - What sources have already been checked?
    - Is the information needed in a special format (in a spreadsheet file, for example)?
    - For quantitative data, what units of measurement are preferred?
    - What deadlines do we need to meet?

- **Once you think you understand the question** and the parameters of the research, confirm this understanding by stating it back to the requester.

    Clarifying the request is particularly important when doing research for someone else but, even for self-directed research, reflection before action can save you time and produce better results. When doing research to meet your own needs, it is easy to start with a vague notion of your information need, move immediately to throwing a few words into a general search engine, and from there go to sorting through hundreds of irrelevant search results. If you can make a clear statement of the underlying problem or goal, you will be able to focus your research on relevant and actionable information.

§1.2 Map Your Research Strategy

Where should you start? What obstacles can you anticipate?

- If there are several questions to be answered, which should be researched first?
- What are the likely information sources? A database on the Internet? An in-house expert? (You will learn much more about information sources throughout this book.)
- Which sources does your audience consider authoritative?

- Do you have access to the sources you need? Do you need to call an expert who resides in a different time zone? Does the database require a paid subscription?

§1.3 Be Aware of Copyright or Other Restrictions on Re-use

If you need to copy someone else's work in whole or in part, determine if you have legal permission to do so. For guidance, consult:

- "Copyright Basics" from the U.S. Copyright Office, *<www.copyright.gov/circs/circ1.pdf>*

- "A Practical Guide to Copyright Compliance" from the Copyright Clearance Center, Inc., *<www.copyright.com/Services/CorporateGuide/index3.htm>*

- "Frequently Asked Questions About Copyright: Issues Affecting the U.S. Government" from CENDI.gov, *<www.cendi.gov/publications/04-8copyright.html>*

- Any license or other terms of use agreement accompanying the source

An alternative to U.S. copyright, called the Creative Commons License, is increasingly popular. To learn about Creative Commons License terms, see *<http://creativecommons.org/about/licenses/>*.

§1.4 Have a Plan for Documenting Your Work and Research Results

Documenting the steps taken will help you to avoid duplication of effort, support any conclusions you make, allow others to consult your sources, and facilitate ongoing research or offshoot projects.

- Make a log of phone calls made, including date, contact name, and phone number.

- For web research, bookmarking the web addresses consulted may not be enough of a record, because the content of a web site can change. Print or save images of the documentation you need. A variety of products are available to help you capture and annotate your web research, save and organize research notes, and share the notes with a group. Research organizers, each with a different array of capabilities, include:

- Diigo, *<www.diigo.com>*
- Evernote, *<http://evernote.com>*
- Ubernote, *<www.ubernote.com>*
- Zotero, *<www.zotero.org>*

(Our mention of these specific products does not constitute an endorsement; there are many other products in this dynamic market.)

For all resources used, gather at least enough information to cite the source so that someone else can find it again. Depending on the discipline you are working in or the institution you are working for, there may be a formal citation style that you are expected to follow. Most current style guides include information on citing online sources. Consult these web sites for more information:

- "Chicago-Style Citation Quick Guide" from Chicago Manual of Style Online, *<www.chicagomanualofstyle.org/tools_citationguide.html>*
- "Resources for Documenting Sources in the Disciplines" from Purdue University, *<http://owl.english.purdue.edu/owl/resource/585/02/>*
- *The Bluebook*, 18th edition, *<www.legalbluebook.com>* for American legal citation style. (See § 4.40 for more information.)
- "Harvard Business School Citation Guide" from Harvard Business School, *<www.library.hbs.edu/guides/citationguide.pdf>*

§1.10 Research Is a Process

What can make research fascinating, and frustrating, is that it seldom goes down a straight path. It is often difficult to know whether you have taken the detour that will lead to the pot of gold, the one that will get you mired in a swamp, or the one that appears to be the sensible choice but that will in fact keep you unwittingly just out of sight of that pot of gold. Here are a few points to keep in mind as you work on a research project:

- Don't stop at the tip of the iceberg. When you use one search engine and conclude your research after skimming through the first ten results, chances are you are missing something. In this book, we supply you with a rich variety of places to begin your research and tips for searching online.

- Review initial research results to see how they can help you expand or narrow your search. If you find a policy paper that is on-topic, read the footnotes to find the resources the author used; those resources may also be useful to you. If you read a newspaper article about your topic, investigate any experts the article quotes; they may have published unique information of interest. Your initial search results may also show you new terminology you can use to refine your next search.

- Don't stop if all you find confirms what you already know without adding to your knowledge. Take a skeptical approach to early assumptions you and others may have made about what you will find. Be a contrarian. If, after your research, you find that the most authoritative sources support your original argument, your argument will be made that much stronger.

- Recognize warning signs. If you are using a large search engine, such as Google, and finding little relevant information on your topic, perhaps you are using the wrong words, or not constructing the search properly. If you are not finding current information about what you know to be an ongoing issue, perhaps you are searching in the wrong place.

- Know when to ask for help. If you are doing research for someone else, recognize that going back to the requestor for clarification or for a status check on what you have found so far may ultimately result in finding the right information faster. If you are researching for yourself, recognize when you may have to take a few steps back to understand your topic better. You may need to consult an encyclopedia entry, a basic treatise, your firm's librarian, or an expert you know.

- Know when to stop. An absolute deadline often tells you when to stop but, if you are juggling multiple projects, you have to make that time management judgment for yourself. Are you beginning to find the same policy papers or university experts cited in reliable sources? Do the experts, for the most part, agree on the same basic data or principles? Keep in mind the 'tip of the iceberg' advice above, but recognize that you can stop when you have relevant information from authoritative sources.

§1.99 Chapter Summary and Review Questions

Chapter Summary

Research benefits from preparation. To prepare: identify the precise question you are trying to answer; map a research strategy; be aware of copyright or other restrictions on re-use; and have a plan for documenting your work and research results. Once the research has begun, recognize when to modify your strategy and when to stop researching.

Review Questions

- You have been asked to "get everything you can find on the topic of health-care reform." What questions can you ask the requestor in order to make this a more manageable and useful research project?
- What are some signs that it is time to stop researching?

Chapter Two

Going Beyond Google

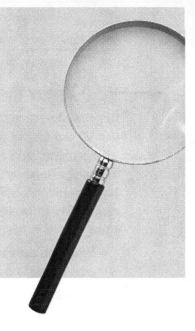

General search engines have quickly become the default information resource for many people. But they are not always the best choice and—even when we do use them—we often are not using them optimally or with a full understanding of how they work.

This chapter offers information and guidance on using search engines and on searching in general.

§2.0 Know the Full Range of Information Sources

General search engines—such as Google or Yahoo!—are so easy to use that it can be tempting to try to use them for any research problem, whether appropriate or not. Remember the old saying, "to the man with a hammer, everything looks like a nail"? Efficient research makes use of the best resources for the problem, and the best is not always a general search engine. The full spectrum of research resources includes, but is not limited to:

- Free web resources sponsored by educational, advocacy, government, commercial, and other entities.
- For-fee commercial online services such as CQ.com or LexisNexis.
- "Offline" resources—people and print.

This book describes information resources of all sorts, including general search engines.

§2.1 Major Search Engines

TIP: *Try the advanced search option, if one is available. The menu options on advanced search screens often make it easier for you to construct an effective search.*

AllPlus

<www.allplus.com>

AllPlus searches the Ask.com, Google, Live Search, and Yahoo! Search engine databases at once.

Bing

<www.bing.com>

Microsoft's Web search engine organizes search results by category, suggests related searches, and provides image and video search. Bing also features customized sections for shopping, travel, health, and local search.

Google

<www.google.com>

Google is an extremely popular search engine. It is fast, powerful, and has a simple interface. Behind the simple interface, Google is capable of complex searching. See the Advanced Search options screen. A site called

§2.2 Limitations of General Search Engines

General search engines help researchers find the web addresses, or URLs, needed to retrieve specific web sites. General search engines serve as indexes to a lot of the popular information available via the web. But searchers should be aware of their limitations:

- **Search engines cover only a fraction of the content on the web.** If a search engine does not find information you need, you can't conclude that the information is not on the web. The web is simply too large and dynamic for any search engine to index it comprehensively. Some information, such as that on sites requiring user-registration or behind a corporate firewall, is off-limits to search engines.

- **Search engines do not necessarily have the most current information.** Because it takes time to find and index information on the web, search engines do not provide the most recent news or changes to web content.

- **There is no quality filter for the information on the web.** Content of any kind—factual, scholarly, satirical, deceptive— resides on the web. Much of it has no label or clear indicator of purpose, target audience, or author credentials. Sifting through and evaluating the varied content delivered by general search engines consumes valuable time.

- **Search results are subject to manipulation both by the search engine and by those who post content to the web.** Because searches often result in hundreds or thousands of results, the results near the top are the ones that most people consult. Due to the open nature of the web, anyone from marketers to pranksters may affect what gets ranked near the top.

Soople (<*www.soople.com*>)—which is not affiliated with Google—makes it even easier to take advantage of these advanced search options.

Yahoo! Search

<*http://search.yahoo.com*>

Yahoo! Search is probably the closest rival to Google. Like Google, it offers an advanced search and special features such as a search for images on the web.

§2.3 Handy Guides

InfoPeople Search Engine Guides:

- **Best Search Tools**, *<http://infopeople.org/search/tools.html>*
- **Best Search Tools Chart**, *<http://infopeople.org/search/chart.html>*

These concise guides to search engine features are provided by InfoPeople, a project of the state of California to assist its libraries.

§2.10 Know How to Start from Scratch

Researching in a subject area that is new to you can be particularly challenging. You may not be familiar with the vocabulary or jargon of the field. You may lack the expertise needed to evaluate general search engine results, and you may not know where else to begin. The following web sites can be effective finding aids (resources that help you find the sources you need to do your work).

Several of these resources are provided by academic libraries. Library web sites often provide selective lists of books, databases, and web sites in areas of interest to students and faculty. Access to some links may be limited to the campus users; this is usually indicated with a note or symbol.

§2.11 Starting Points on the Web

General Subject Guides:

- Delicious, *<http://delicious.com>*. Delicious is a social bookmarking site owned by Yahoo! Inc. Users bookmark their favorite sites to share with others. The result is a database of popular web sites. Search on a topic, such as biodiesel or food safety, to find the most popular web sites on the topic.

- Intute, *<www.intute.ac.uk>*. This extensive directory of research-quality web sites links to online information in all disciplines related to social sciences, science and technology, health and life sciences, and arts and humanities. The site is maintained by a group of subject experts from British universities.

- The Internet Public Library (IPL), *<www.ipl.org>*, is a directory of selected web sites on topics such as business, education, health, and government. IPL also has research guides and a directory of links to newspapers and magazines online. The site is sponsored by Drexel University. (IPL is planning a name change; this web address should forward to the new site.)

Public Policy and Government:

- University of Michigan Documents Center, *<www.lib.umich.edu/ govdocs/>*. This library site is an extensive guide to information resources on federal, state, and international government topics.

- USA.gov, *<www.usa.gov>*. Administered by the U.S. General Services Administration, USA.gov is the official web portal for the U.S. government. Web links are organized by topic, such as Science and Technology. USA.gov also has a government web search engine.

Law:

- FindLaw, *<www.findlaw.com>*. This free web site from the Thomson publishing company provides background information and resource guides for legal topics, with sections tailored to the public and legal professionals.

- Georgetown University Law "Find It Fast" Page, *<www.ll.george town.edu/find/>*. The Georgetown Law Library's guides to books, databases, and web sites cover a wide variety of legal topics.

Business:

- globalEDGE, *<http://globaledge.msu.edu>*. Managed by the International Business Center at Michigan State University, this site provides practical business information and recommended web sites for specific industries, countries, and U.S. states.

- Best of the Business Web, *<www.jjhill.org/research_online/best_ of_the_business_web.cfm>*. Business information specialists at the James J. Hill Reference Library have selected useful web sites on numerous business-related topics.

§2.12 Starting Points in Print

- *e-Government and Web Directory: U.S. Federal Government Online* (Lanham, MD: Bernan Press). Extensive guide to federal government web sites. Updated annually. See *<www.bernanpress.com>*.

- *Washington Information Directory* (Washington: CQ Press).
  A guide to Washington contacts from federal agencies, Congress,
  and private interest groups. Updated annually; also available online
  for a fee. See *<www.cqpress.com>*.

§2.20 Know What You Are Searching

§ 2.30 covers *how* to search. But, before you begin searching, it is important to understand *what* you are searching. You wouldn't look in a wood-
workers' tool catalog for a good deal on the latest MP3 player, would you?
Of course not. An inappropriate choice of a web database is not always so
obvious.

Some examples:

- The Library of Congress THOMAS website, *<http://thomas.loc.gov>*,
  is the first place many researchers look for congressional information,
  but it is not the place to look for the transcripts of congressional
  hearings. (The transcripts may be available from the committee,
  from the Government Printing Office, or from commercial sources.)

- Contrary to popular belief, the Library of Congress does not have
  a copy of every book published. If you search for a book in the
  Library of Congress catalog, *<http://catalog.loc.gov>*, and do not
  find it, that does not mean the book was not published.

§2.21 How Do You Learn about a Database's Content?

✔ Read all available information the database provides,
such as any "help" or "about" pages on the web site.

✔ Conduct test searches to plumb the depths of the database. For
example, if a person or company is not listed in a database, try
searching on the name of a similar person or company or the name
of a very famous person or company. Test searches such as these
can help you discover limitations in a database's coverage.

✔ Call the sponsor of the database or others skilled in using the data.

✔ Take training classes offered for the databases you will need to
use often.

§2.31 What Do You Need to Know before You Search?

Some of the questions you will want to have answered are:

✔ How do I search on a phrase, such as "red cross"?

✔ Does the search engine find word variations—such as "vote," "voter," and "voting"—or do I need to search on each of these variations?

✔ What additional search options are available on the "advanced search" page?

✔ Are there any special searches—such as searching on numbers or legal citations—that are handled differently?

§2.32 Help!

To learn how to use the database, read the help. This is what the experts do. Examples of search engine help:

• **Google Help: Cheat Sheet,** *<www.google.com/help/cheatsheet.html>*

• **Yahoo! Help,** *<http://help.yahoo.com/l/us/yahoo/search/>*

§2.30 Know How to Search the Database

Many web sites offer the same blank search box, but the way each processes your search words can vary.

Type the phrase **red cross** into Google, and your top results will include the phrase **red cross**, with the words next to each other and in that order—American Red Cross, International Committee of the Red Cross, British Red Cross, etc.

Type the same phrase into the *Congressional Record* on GPO Access, *<www.gpoaccess.gov>*, and your search may find a statement about "National Wear Red Day" that uses the word **red** many times but never uses the word cross.

Why? On GPO Access, you must type a phrase in quotes to ensure that your results include that exact phrase. If you type just those two words in Google, the search engine assumes that results with the exact phrase are most relevant and puts them at the top. Google also assumes that both words must be in the most relevant search results.

The new system due to replace GPO Access—GPO FDsys, <*www. fdsys.gov*>—will look for both words, just as Google does.

§2.33 Planning and Conducting an Online Search

✔ **Envision the answer.** What would the answer to your question look like? Will it be technical or popular literature, or a set of numerical data? Who would write or speak about your topic? An advocacy group, a political scientist, an industry specialist, a local journalist, or a congressional committee? Thinking broadly about these questions will help you choose a source to search and to come up with effective words for your search.

✔ **Use more than one search engine or online database.** Unless you have a very narrow question, such as, "who is the Comptroller General of the United States," you will often benefit from searching more than one source. This is particularly true when using general search engines, because no single search engine covers the entire web and each indexes some material that the others do not.

✔ **Learn from the results of your first search.** Searching is an iterative process. Review your initial search results and see if there are words you should add or drop.

✔ **Try variations on your first search.** Even slight variations will almost always produce different results in a general search engine or large database.

✔ **Think of common synonyms or alternate terms.** For example, the concept *global warming* might also be expressed as *global change, climate change,* or *greenhouse effect.*

✔ **Eliminate ambiguity in your search.** *Turkey* may be a country or a bird. *China* may be a country or a porcelain material. If you cannot come up with a less ambiguous alternate word, try adding other words to limit to the sense of the word that you intend; for example, *turkey dinner* or *turkey hunting.* Another option is to choose an online source that is limited in subject coverage. For example, a search on *turkey* in the State Department web site will find background and policy news on the country of Turkey, with only a few irrelevant results involving the annual White House

§2.34 Constructing a Search with Boolean Operators

Searching in some online databases requires the use of "Boolean operators" (AND, OR, NOT), named for nineteenth-century logician George Boole. This guide contains explanations and examples of Boolean searching.

AND	OR	NOT
Both words must be present.	Either word, or both, should be present.	The word must not be present.
Makes the search more specific by requiring that *all* of your search words must be in the result; for example: **cats AND dogs**	Broadens the search. Best used for synonyms or like terms; for example: **cats OR felines** **IRS OR "internal revenue service"**	Helps to narrow the search by excluding some results; for example: **pets NOT cats**
On the web, AND is sometimes expressed as the menu option: Find results with *all of the words.*	On the web, OR is sometimes expressed as the menu option: Find results with *any of the words.*	On the web, NOT is sometimes expressed as the menu option: Find results with *none of the words.*
This search: **liberty AND death**	This search: **liberty OR death**	This search: **liberty NOT death**
Will find:	Will find:	Will find:
#1 Is life so dear, or peace so sweet, as to be purchased at the price of chains and slavery? Forbid it, Almighty God! I know not what course others may take; but as for me, give me **liberty** or give me **death**!	#1 Is life so dear, or peace so sweet, as to be purchased at the price of chains and slavery? Forbid it, Almighty God! I know not what course others may take; but as for me, give me **liberty** or give me **death**! #2 Four score and seven years ago our fathers brought forth on this continent a new nation, conceived in **liberty** and dedicated to the proposition that all men are created equal.	#2 Four score and seven years ago our fathers brought forth on this continent a new nation, conceived in **liberty** and dedicated to the proposition that all men are created equal.

pardoning of a Thanksgiving turkey. A third option is to use advanced search techniques to exclude results with the sense you do not intend, such as excluding any results with the word *Thanksgiving*.

✔ **Critically evaluate the results of your searches.** Can you identify the source of the information they provide? Is the information current and reasonably complete? Does the information lead to other promising sources?

§2.35 Searching and Limiting When You Get Too Much

The ideal search would find only information relevant to your information need and, if desired, all information relevant to your information need. Search tools are not sophisticated enough to achieve this, but various search techniques can help improve the usefulness of your search results.

✔ **Search on highly specific words and phrases.** Make your search terms as specific as possible. For example, "human anatomy" is more specific than "anatomy," which is more specific than "biology."

✔ **Limit your search to the most relevant section of the online offerings, if possible.** For example, searchers looking for a book on Amazon.com will be more efficient if they limit the search at the outset to just the "Books" section of Amazon.

✔ **Limit the parameters of your search, using the options on advanced search screens and elsewhere.** General search engines and other databases usually have options to limit your search results by language, type of document, publication date range, and other parameters.

§2.36 Dates

Use caution when limiting your search by publication date range. General search engines are often not able to distinguish true publication dates for web documents. Also, our recollections of when we saw a news article or heard a speech tend to be surprisingly inaccurate.

§2.37 Example for Limiting When You Get Too Much

Library of Congress Online Catalog

The Library of Congress has voluminous collections of material in languages other than English. Also, many of the items in its catalog are not books, but maps, sound recordings, sheet music, etc. If you are interested in English-language books, select those limits from the outset. ❶

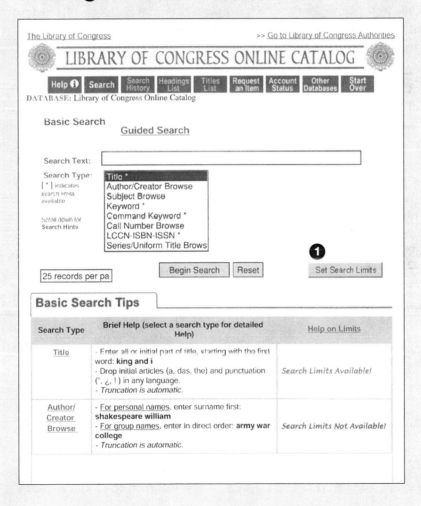

§2.38 Learn from the Pros

Experts from research and computer-related fields maintain web sites to track developments in search engines, test search engine performance, and develop resources and tutorials for search engine users. You can improve and keep your skills up-to-date by taking advantage of any of these expert sites:

Finding Information on the Internet: A Tutorial

<www.lib.berkeley.edu/TeachingLib/Guides/Internet/FindInfo.html>

This web site features search strategy tips, comparisons of top search engines, and other useful Internet search help. The library for the University of California at Berkeley maintains the site.

Pandia Search Central

<www.pandia.com>

Pandia includes a directory of general and specialized search engines and a search tutorial. The Pandia email newsletter and blog provide updates on search engine developments. Per and Susanne Koch of Norway own and edit Pandia.

Resource Shelf "Search Tools" News

<www.resourceshelf.com/category/source-file/resources/search-tools/>

Resource Shelf, *<www.resourceshelf.com>*, reports on web research news in a number of categories. The "search tools" category follows general search engine news. Free Pint Limited, a British firm, publishes Resource Shelf.

§2.40 Review Search Results Critically

So far, we have discussed finding information resources and conducting an online search. But the research process does not end there. Evaluating the information you have found is the next part of the story.

§2.41 Evaluating Information

✔ **What is the source of the information?** Is it readily identified? Does the source have any bias or motivation for bias? If the information is second-hand, find the original source.

§2.42 Fact-Checking Resources

- The book *How to Lie with Statistics* (New York: W.W. Norton, 1993) is a classic, written in 1954 and reissued many times. It is a guide to understanding how others may use statistics in a misleading fashion.

- **PolitiFact** (*<www.politifact.com>*) launched during the 2008 U.S. presidential campaign, is similar to FactCheck.org. In 2009, they changed their focus from the campaign to fact-checking government officials, special interest groups, and "other players" in national government. PolitiFact is a project of the *St. Petersburg Times* and *Congressional Quarterly*.

- The Annenberg Public Policy Center's **FactCheck.org** (*<www.factcheck.org>*) web site monitors, as they state, "the factual accuracy of what is said by major U.S. political players in the form of TV ads, debates, speeches, interviews, and news releases."

- The book *unSpun: finding facts in a world of disinformation* (New York: Random House, 2007) provides fact-finding guidance from Brooks Jackson and Kathleen Hall Jamieson, the creators of FactCheck.org.

- **Snopes.com Urban Legend Reference Pages** (*<www.snopes.com>*) provides extensive background information on popular rumors, misinformation, strange news stories, and the type of fallacies or half-truths that travel quickly on the Internet.

✔ **Can the information be verified independently?** Factual errors can occur even in typically authoritative sources. Find a second or third source to corroborate.

✔ **Is the information current?** If it may have been affected by newer developments, can you search for such news?

✔ **Is the information complete?** Think critically. You may never find "all" relevant information, but do you have the critical pieces you need for your purpose?

§2.43 Evaluating a Web Site

✔ **Determine the author or sponsor of the web site.** Is the author clearly identified? Does the site provide information on its sponsor and how to contact them? Is the sponsor an individual

§2.44 Web Tools for Evaluating Web Sites

Find out who links to the web site and what they say about it. Many search engines provide a feature, usually on the engine's advanced search page, that lets you find web sites that link to a specified site. The results can often provide clues about the site's popularity and whether reputable organizations find the site to be trustworthy.

Example on Google: link:www.opensecrets.org

"Whois" is an old Internet tool designed to provide information on who has registered a particular Internet web address, or domain. There are many "whois" tools available. Two to try are DomainTools Whois, *<www.domaintools.com>*, and Allwhois, *<http://allwhois.com/>*. Unfortunately, the accuracy and completeness of the domain registration information cannot be guaranteed—no matter which "whois" service you use—because it is up to the domain name owners themselves to provide the information.

or an institution? While there are exceptions to the rule, web sites sponsored by reputable institutions are generally more trustworthy than individual efforts. The institution must maintain its reputation and may have the resources to edit information for quality and accuracy. If you are not familiar with the identified author or sponsor, do further research.

✔ **Identify the purpose of the web site.** Is it clearly stated? Does it have a particular advocacy position or something to sell? Determine if the web site is non-partisan. Commercial, government, policy, political, and educational sites tend to have differing goals. This does not mean that the information one provides is any less worthy than the other, but you should be aware of the goals of the site or its sponsors.

✔ **Review the site's overall information quality.** Is information current? Check the date of the copyright statement and the currency of any press releases. Are links maintained? Is the source of information documented?

✔ **Assess the site's suitability to your research.** Does it have the required level of detail or the range of information needed? Does it appear to be a stable source you can refer to in the future?

✔ **Review the quality of the site's "web practices."** Does the web site follow good practices, such as not letting its own links go dead?

§2.50 Stay Informed

 The Internet offers many ways to have information updates sent to you automatically. The sections below cover current awareness resources for information from and about government.

§2.51 Email Alert Services: A Selected Sample

The following free services deliver updates directly to your email account once you have requested a subscription.

- *Federal Register* table of contents. Subscribe via *<http://listserv. access.gpo.gov>*; click on "online mailing list archives," then look for FEDREGTOC-L.

- Public Laws Electronic Notification Service. Subscribe via *<www.archives.gov/federal-register/laws/updates.html>* for notification of public law numbers as they are assigned by the National Archives Office of the Federal Register.

- Government Accountability Office (GAO) Topic Updates. Subscribe via *<www.gao.gov/subscribe/index.php>* to receive notification of new GAO reports in your issue area.

Many other congressional and executive offices provide email alert services. USA.gov provides a partial list at *<http://apps.gsa.gov/Common SubscriptionService.php>*.

§2.52 Avoid Information Overload

Too much information delivered to you automatically every day can be worse than none at all if it distracts from your primary mission, or if crucial data gets lost among the not-so-crucial data.

When you subscribe to a news update service or discussion list, learn how to unsubscribe and save the instructions for doing so.

Subscribe cautiously and weed subscriptions ruthlessly. Does the service duplicate news you get elsewhere? Is its coverage too broad in scope? Is there a more manageable source for the same information?

§2.53 Blogs: A Selected Sample

Blogs, short for "web logs," are web sites that are regularly updated with news or opinion. They usually consist of daily entries, with the most recent entries displayed prominently. The typical blog also has archived entries and links to related blogs. While many blogs deal in rumor or personal issues, the following examples provide useful information for the Washington researcher:

- beSpacific, <*www.bespacific.com*>, covers law and technology news. It is written by law librarian Sabrina Pacifici.

§2.54 Selected RSS Readers

- **Google Reader**, <*http://reader.google.com*>, is a popular and free web site for reading RSS feeds.
- **Newsgator Technologies**, <*www.newsgator.com*>, offers several different RSS readers, for free and for fee. One of their popular free readers is NewGator Online, <*www.newsgator.com/individuals/*>.

- ResourceShelf's DocuTicker, <*www.docuticker.com*>, announces new studies and reports from government agencies, foundations, think tanks, and other organizations. It is compiled by a team of research librarians.

- SCOTUSblog, <*www.scotusblog.com*>, reports on the U.S. Supreme Court. It is sponsored by the law firm Akin Gump.

- Washington Wire, <*http://blogs.wsj.com/washwire/*>, from the *Wall Street Journal*'s WSJ.com web site, is one of many news blogs reporting on the Washington scene. The blog entries often link directly to the documents or news reports discussed.

§2.55 RSS News Feeds: A Selected Sample

RSS stands for "Really Simple Syndication," a format for information distribution. News services, government agencies, and other publishers are increasing their use of RSS for distribution of news updates independent of email. RSS news feeds are often indicated by the orange RSS logo: Examples can be found at the following sites:

- Consumer Product Safety Commission provides an RSS feed of product recalls and safety news via <*www.cpsc.gov/cpscpub/prerel/rss.html*>.

- Department of Defense news, contract announcements, speech transcripts, and other RSS news feeds are available via *<www.defenselink.mil/news/rss/>*.
- Yahoo! News offers news feeds by category, such as politics or science news. Users can also create a customized news feed based on a word search. Yahoo! offers detailed information at *<http://news.yahoo.com/rss>*.

The federal government's USA.gov site provides a directory of government RSS feeds at *<www.usa.gov/Topics/Reference_Shelf/Libraries/RSS_Library.shtml>*.

§2.56 Commercial Online Services

Many commercial online information services provide the ability to receive customized news updates. The services typically require a subscription. For more information, contact the companies directly. Online services providing such capabilities include:

- CQ.com, *<www.cq.com>*, for legislative news.
- GalleryWatch, *<www.gallerywatch.com>*, for legislative news.
- LexisNexis, *<www.lexisnexis.com>*, for a wide range of business, legal, and government news.
- Westlaw, *<http://west.thomson.com/store/>*, for a wide range of business, legal, and government news.
- Dow Jones Factiva, *<www.factiva.com>*, for a wide range of business, industry, financial, and general news.

§2.60 Remember, It's Not All Online

Much of the world's knowledge cannot be found in online databases. Your research will often involve talking to experts and insiders (see Chapter 6) and can still involve traveling around town to use paper records.

§2.61 We Have So Many Records That . . .

The National Archives has created this cartoon to illustrate the fact that most of its records cannot be found online:

We have so many records that...

Laid side to side, pages in our holdings would circle the Earth over 57 times! Because of the cost to digitize such a volume of materials, **only a small percentage is available for research online**. Our web site offers tools and guides to help you locate these documents. To complete your research and use the records, you may need to <u>visit us</u>.

Source: *<www.archives.gov/research/>*

§2.99 Chapter Summary and Review Questions

Chapter Summary

General search engines such as Google cover only a portion of the information that is available on the web. Your research will benefit from being aware of a range of search engines and search techniques, as well as online starting points that are not search engines. Managing the flood of information on the web requires techniques for evaluating information and information sources and for staying informed without being overwhelmed.

Review Questions

- Why should you be familiar with more than one search engine?
- How can you make a search more precise if your initial search yields too many irrelevant results?
- How can you assess whether a web site might be a reliable source?

Chapter Three

Legislative Branch Research

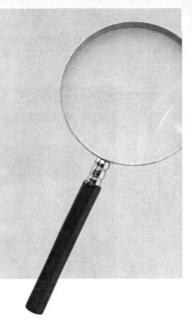

The information resources of the legislative branch consist primarily of the documents of the U.S. Congress. THOMAS (<*http://thomas.loc.gov*>) and GPO Access (<*www.gpoaccess.gov*>), or GPO FDsys (<*www.fdsys. gov*>), along with the web sites of the House (<*www. house.gov*>) and Senate (<*www.senate.gov*>), are the major congressional online services available to the public for free.

The following section has information about basic legislative resources, along with quick reference information related to legislative research. For further reading and much more information on legislative research resources, see *Congressional Deskbook, 5th Edition* (Alexandria, VA: TheCapitol.Net, 2007).

§3.0 Legislative Process Flowchart

Legislation may begin in either chamber.
Similar proposals are often introduced in both chambers.

Measure introduced in the House *§8.20*	Measure introduced in the Senate *§8.20*
Measure referred to committee, which holds hearings and reports measure to the House *§8.30, §8.40, §8.50, §8.60*	Measure referred to committee, which holds hearings and reports measure to the Senate *§8.30, §8.40, §8.50, §8.60*

OR

For important measures, special rule reported by the Rules Committee and adopted by the House *§8.90, §8.100*

Leadership schedules measure for floor consideration *§8.70*	Leadership schedules measure for floor consideration *§8.160, §8.170*
House debates and can amend measure *§8.110, §8.120*	Senate debates and can amend measure *§8.180, §8.190, §8.200, §8.210, §8.220, §8.230*
House passes measure *§8.130, §8.140*	Senate passes measure *§8.240, §8.250*

Measures must pass both the House and the Senate
in identical form before being presented to the President.

One chamber agrees to the other chamber's version *§8.260*	OR	Each chamber appoints Members to a conference committee, which reconciles differences and agrees to a conference report *§8.280*	OR	House and Senate exchange amendments to bill and reach agreement *§8.270*

House approves conference report	Senate approves conference report

Legislation presented to the President.

President signs measure	If President does not sign measure into law within 10 days *§8.290*		President vetoes measure
Measure becomes law	If Congress is in session, measure becomes law	If Congress is not in session, measure does not become law ("pocket veto")	Measure does not become law, unless both chambers override veto by 2/3 majority

Source: § 8.01, *Congressional Deskbook*, <CongressionalDeskbook.com>

§3.10 Quick Reference for Legislative Researchers

§3.11 Types of Legislation

Type	Abbreviation	Brief Description
Simple Resolution	H.Res., S.Res.	Used for administrative matters affecting only the House or only the Senate. Does not go to the other chamber or to the president. Does not have force of law. (The House also uses the H.Res. form for special rules from the Rules Committee.)
Concurrent Resolution	H.Con.Res., S.Con.Res.	Used for administrative matters affecting both chambers. Requires both chambers' approval but not signature of president. Does not have force of law.
Joint Resolution	H.J.Res., S.J.Res.	Similar to a bill, but used for specific purposes, such as proposed amendments to the Constitution. Requires the approval of both chambers and the president. If approved, has the force of law.
Bill	H.R., S.	Legislative proposal requiring approval of both chambers and the president to become law.
Amendment	H.Amdt., S.Amdt.	Text proposed by a member of Congress to change the text of legislation under consideration.

§3.12 Continuing Resolutions

When Congress fails to approve all appropriations bills before the end of the government's fiscal year each October 1, members will often pass what is referred to as a "continuing resolution," making temporary, continuing appropriations. A continuing resolution is not another type of bill. It is an unofficial term. These temporary measures typically are introduced as joint resolutions but may be introduced in other forms.

§3.13 Major Versions of Legislation

Version	Description
As Introduced	The initial version, when a bill or resolution number is assigned.
As Reported	The legislation as amended and reported favorably by committee to the House or Senate.
Engrossed	The legislation as passed by one chamber.
As Received in House As Received in Senate	The version of the legislation when it is accepted for consideration by one chamber or the other.
Enrolled	The final version as passed in identical form by both the House and Senate and sent to the president.

§3.14 Dates of Previous Congresses

A complete list of congressional session dates since 1789 is available from the Clerk of the House web site, at <http://clerk. house.gov/art_history/house_history/Session_Dates/index.html>.

Congress	Dates	Congress	Dates
110	2007–2008	102	1991–1992
109	2005–2006	101	1989–1990
108	2003–2004	100	1987–1988
107	2001–2002	99	1985–1986
106	1999–2000	98	1983–1984
105	1997–1998	97	1981–1982
104	1995–1996	96	1979–1980
103	1993–1994	95	1977–1978

§3.15 Legislative Glossaries

- **Congressional Bills: Glossary**
  <www.gpoaccess.gov/bills/glossary.html>
  Lists and explains the types and versions of legislation.

- **Congressional and Legislative Terms**
  <www.thecapitol.net/glossary>
  Provides an extensive glossary of terms, from "act" to "veto" and beyond.

§3.20 Documents on THOMAS and GPO Access

THOMAS and GPO Access both provide access to the basic documents listed in the table below, albeit in different formats and for different time spans. For current committee hearings, check the committee home pages on the House and Senate web sites; GPO Access provides an incomplete selection of these from 1997 to present, and THOMAS does not have its own hearings database. (Note: The Government Printing Office is transitioning from the GPO Access system to its replacement, GPO FDsys. See § 3.21.)

For more information, see TheCapitol.Net guide at *<congressional documents.com>*. For a more detailed listing of congressional documents online that includes commercial online services, see "Electronic Sources for Federal Legislative History Documents," by Richard J. McKinney of the Law Librarians' Society of Washington, DC, at *<www.llsdc.org/elec-leg-hist-docs/>*.

Content Highlights	THOMAS <http://thomas.loc.gov>	GPO Access <www.gpoaccess.gov>
Committee Reports	1995–present	1995–present
Congressional Record	1989–present	1994–present
Legislative status steps	1973–present	1983–present *(less detail, less current than THOMAS)*
Text of legislation	1989–present	1993–present
Text of public laws	*(THOMAS links to GPO for public laws)*	1995–present

§3.21 GPO Access and the Federal Digital System

The Government Printing Office has operated its electronic document retrieval site, GPO Access, since 1994. GPO Access provides PDF and text versions of documents from the legislative, executive, and judicial branches. It also has a government publications catalog, an online government bookstore, and information on the federal government resources available to you locally through the Federal Depository Library Program, *<www.gpo.gov/libraries/>*.

Because GPO Access uses older technology, word searching operates quite differently than on other popular web sites, such as Google. Be sure to review the quick search tips and search examples provided with every GPO Access database. Here are a few searching tips:

- To search on a phrase, put the phrase in double quotes; for example, "supreme court" or "equal employment opportunity commission".

- Put the word AND between each word or phrase you want to find; for example, "supreme court" AND Hamdi. (For more information, see §§ 2.30 and 2.34.)

- Take advantage of the advanced search option to limit your search by year, Congress, or other available options.

Throughout 2009, GPO will be releasing its databases on a new system called the Federal Digital System, or FDsys, *<www.fdsys.gov>*. GPO will keep GPO Access online until the transition to the new system is complete.

§3.30 THOMAS: Legislative Information on the Internet

<http://thomas.loc.gov>

Scope:
- Summaries and status of legislation, 93rd Congress (1973–1974) to present.
- Full text of legislation (all versions of all bills), 101st Congress (1989–1990) to present.
- *Congressional Record*, full text, 101st Congress (1989–1990) to present.
- Roll call votes, 101st Congress (1989–1990) to present; House votes start with 1990.

- Committee reports (House, Senate, Joint, and Conference), 104th Congress (1995–1996) to present.
- Links to related information, such as the House and Senate floor schedules and committee web sites.
- Charts tracking activity on appropriations legislation (best for Fiscal Year 2002 to present).
- Status of presidential nominations and treaties sent to the Senate for consideration.

Sponsor:

Library of Congress, on behalf of U.S. Congress. (Information in THOMAS is drawn from sources including the House, Senate, Government Printing Office, and Congressional Research Service.)

Description:

The Bill Summary and Status (BSS) database on THOMAS serves as the starting point for finding bills and amendments, and for finding information and documents related to a specific bill—such as debate in the *Congressional Record*, roll call votes, rules under which a bill was considered, and committee reports. BSS has a summary of each bill, written by the Congressional Research Service; a status section tracking the steps the bill has taken in the legislative process; and links to any closely related bills or amendments. **BSS is found under Bills and Resolutions.**

The Bill Text database on THOMAS allows you to search on every word in a bill. Bills found in this database also link to the complementary information available in the Bill Summary and Status database. **Bill Text is found under Bills and Resolutions.**

Other databases on THOMAS, such as the *Congressional Record*, are useful when looking for content that is not necessarily linked to a known bill.

THOMAS Tips:

- Most THOMAS databases are updated within twenty-four to forty-eight hours.
- The *Congressional Record* can be particularly difficult to search. If the date is known, try "Browse Daily Issues." To search by topic or a person's name, use "Keyword Index." Note: the Index has a two-week delay.

When searching THOMAS to:	Use:
• Get information about a bill • Track progress of a bill • Find bills sponsored by a certain member of Congress • Find a bill number when you have some information (for example, sponsor and topic of the bill) • Get a list of vetoed bills	Summary and Status Information See § 2.32 **②**
• Get a copy of a bill when you know the bill number • Search the full text of bills	Bill Text See § 2.32 **①**
• Get a committee report, when report number is known • Get a committee report, when the number of the reported bill is known	Committee Reports See § 2.31 **②**
• Find *Congressional Record* statements on a bill	Summary and Status Information (status links to *Congressional Record*) See § 2.32 **②**
• Find *Congressional Record* statements on a topic	*Congressional Record* See § 2.31 **③**

- When researching appropriations legislation, it is usually faster to go directly to the Appropriations Bills chart rather than search in other THOMAS databases. See § 3.40.
- Bill Text provides copies of bills in an HTML outline format. It links to "GPO's PDF" (an Adobe Acrobat format copy from the Government Printing Office) that is formatted like the print copy and can be easier to read. It also links to a "Printer Friendly" display, the full bill in HTML format, which can be easier to bring into word-processing programs. Additionally, Bill Text provides an XML format that is useful to other web publishers.
- The Bill Text database does not include the *public law* version of a bill. Instead, it carries all versions of the bill as it progresses, up

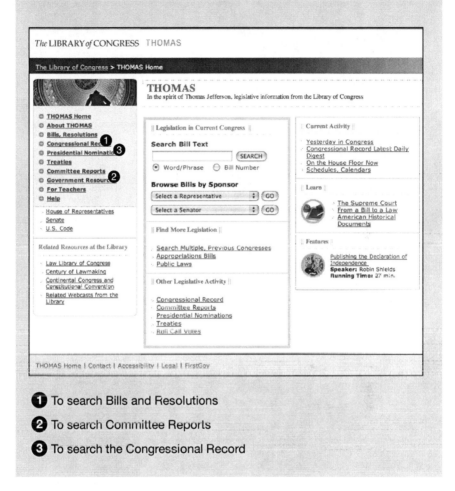

§3.31 Thomas Home Page

1 To search Bills and Resolutions

2 To search Committee Reports

3 To search the Congressional Record

to and including the *enrolled* version. The enrolled version is the version sent to the president for signature. The public law version adds the public law number, *Statutes at Large* citation, and date signed into law. To find the full text of the public law version, use the Public Laws database on THOMAS.

Word Searching:

- THOMAS will automatically search for information in which your search words appear exactly as you typed them. There is no need to use "quotes" to indicate a phrase.

§3.32 Thomas Bills and Resolutions Search Page

1 To search the full text of Bills and Resolutions

2 To search only the Summary Abstracts and Status of Bills and Resolutions

- THOMAS will also show you results in which all of your search words appear, no matter the order.
- The advanced search screens for Bill Text and for Bill Summary and Status allow you to select whether you want to search for the words as you typed them or to also search for "variants" of those words. For example, if "variants" is selected, your search on *tax* will also find any occurrences of *taxes, taxing,* or *taxation.*

§3.40 **Appropriations Legislation**

In each session of each Congress, appropriations bills are some of the most complex and most closely watched legislation. Your research is made much easier by a chart maintained on the THOMAS web site. See the partial sample below for an example for Fiscal Year 2003. For Fiscal Year 2009, go to <*http://thomas.loc.gov/home/approp/app09.html*>.

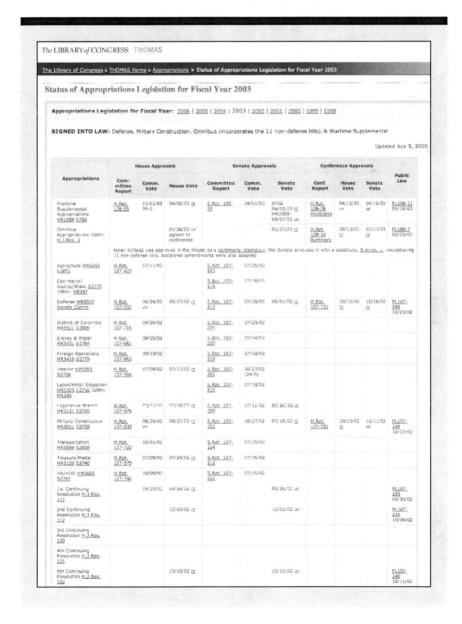

§3.41 Appropriations Committees and Subcommittees

For several decades, Congress considered thirteen regular appropriations acts developed by thirteen parallel subcommittees; each regular appropriations act was developed by the relevant House and Senate Appropriations subcommittee. Realignment of the Appropriations subcommittees in the 109th Congress reduced the number to ten in the House and twelve in the Senate, resulting in subcommittees (and regular appropriations acts) that in some cases were no longer parallel. Further realignment in the 110th Congress resulted in twelve subcommittees in each committee and restored parallelism between them. In some cases, subcommittee jurisdictions were not the same in the 110th Congress as they had been before realignment occurred. The current Appropriations subcommittees are as follows:

- Agriculture, Rural Development, Food and Drug Administration, and Related Agencies
- Commerce, Justice, Science, and Related Agencies
- Defense
- Energy and Water Development
- Financial Services and General Government
- Homeland Security
- Interior, Environment, and Related Agencies
- Labor, Health and Human Services, Education, and Related Agencies
- Legislative Branch
- Military Construction, Veterans Affairs, and Related Agencies
- State, Foreign Operations, and Related Programs
- Transportation, and Housing and Urban Development, and Related Agencies

Source: § 9.82, *Congressional Deskbook, <CongressionalDeskbook.com>*

 ## §3.42 Appropriations Conference Committee Reports

In order for a bill to be sent to the president for his approval or veto, the House and Senate must pass the bill in identical form. For most complex legislation, Congress uses a conference committee to resolve differences between the House and Senate versions. The regular appropriations bills are particularly complex measures, and they almost

§3.43 Limitations, Earmarks, and General Provisions

In addition to appropriating specific dollar amounts, appropriations and their accompanying reports contain numerous other provisions that affect how federal departments and agencies spend appropriations. The principal categories of these provisions include the following:

- **Limitation**—language in legislation or in legislative documents that restricts the availability of an appropriation by limiting its use or amount.

- **Earmark**—a set-aside within an appropriation for a specific purpose that might be included either in legislation or in legislative documents.

- **Directive**—an instruction, probably in a legislative document, to an agency concerning the manner in which an appropriation is to be administered.

- **General Provision**—policy guidance on spending included in an appropriations measure; it may affect some or all appropriation accounts in the measure or even have government-wide application; it may also be one-time or permanent.

Appropriations measures might also contain *riders,* legislative provisions that are included in appropriations measures despite House and Senate rules discouraging the practice.

Source: § 9.81, *Congressional Deskbook,* <*CongressionalDeskbook.com*>

always go through a conference committee. (See the legislative process flowchart at § 3.0 for the place of the conference committee in the legislative process.)

Conference committees issue their agreement in what is commonly referred to as a "conference report." In fact, this document is a combination of two distinct documents: the conference report and the conference managers' statement (also called the joint explanatory statement). Together, these two documents are properly referred to as the "conference papers." The report contains the negotiated legislative language, while the managers' statement is a plain English explanation of each part of the agreement.

The managers' statement is particularly important for legislative researchers because it may contain provisions that are not included in the actual text of the appropriations bill. For example, the managers' statement in the conference papers (H.Rpt. 109-188) for the Interior-Environment-Related Agencies 2006 appropriations bill (H.R. 2361, 109th Cong.) spells out that $640,000 of the appropriations are to be used for re-striping and sealing the Natchez Trace Parkway; the Parkway is not specifically mentioned in the language of the bill.

§ 3.43 provides more information on special provisions that may or may not appear in the text of the legislation.

 # §3.50 **Monitoring Legislative Information: Alert Services**

Free and paid subscription alert services can be used to automatically monitor databases, news sources, and web sites and deliver any updates to the subscriber. Typically, the updates are delivered to the subscriber's email account. A relatively new format is RSS (Really Simple Syndication, see § 2.55), which allows subscribers to receive updates independent of an email account. Instead, updates can be viewed with RSS news reader software, on the web, or on a handheld communication device.

The following selective list of alert services focuses on tracking and monitoring legislation and policy developments.

Congressional Sources

Leadership and Committees

- The *Daily WhipLine* is available from the House Majority Whip. *WhipLine* identifies bills expected to be considered on the House floor. Subscribe to email updates via *<http://majoritywhip.house.gov/daily_whipline/>*. The Senate does not have an exact equivalent.

- *Whip Notice* and *Whipping Post* are issued by the House Republican Whip. Subscribe via *<http://republicanwhip.house.gov>*. The Senate does not have an exact equivalent.

- The Republican Cloakroom web site, *<http://repcloakroom.house.gov>*, has RSS feeds of daily and weekly floor schedule updates.

- The House Rules Committee, *<http://rules.house.gov/>*, maintains an RSS feed with news, notices of committee actions, and copies of special rules as they are issued.

- Some committee web sites provide email alert services via the committee home page. The offerings vary from committee to

§3.51 Recorded Congressional Information

Some congressional and related information is regularly updated on telephone recordings.

House of Representatives Floor Schedule Information:

Democratic Recording (advance schedule), 202-225-1600

Democratic Recording (current proceedings), 202-225-7400

Republican Recording (advance schedule), 202-225-2020

Republican Recording (current proceedings), 202-225-7430

Senate Floor Schedule Information:

Democratic Recording, 202-224-8541

Republican Recording, 202-224-8601

Government Printing Office:

New Congressional Publications, 202-512-1809

White House Executive Clerk:

Status of Bills Received, 202-456-2226

Office of the Federal Register:

New Public Law Numbers, 202-741-6043

Source: § 11.15, *Congressional Deskbook*, *<CongressionalDeskbook.com>*

committee, but they often include schedule updates and press releases. Some provide alerts limited to a specific topic or topics covered by the committee.

Congressional Agencies

- The Library of Congress THOMAS site provides an RSS feed for copies of the Daily Digest section of the *Congressional Record*. The feed address is *<http://thomas.loc.gov/home/rss/dd.xml>*.

- The Congressional Budget Office (CBO) alert service notifies subscribers about new CBO reports. Subscribe via *<www.cbo.gov/listserver/>*.

- The Government Accountability Office (GAO) provides several email alert services, all available via *<www.gao.gov/subscribe/>*. The daily and monthly alert services send email messages with links to GAO reports and testimony released in the previous day or over the course

§3.60 From Bills to Laws: Documents and Information Resources

Legislation is introduced, debated, amended, and passed by Congress.

The final version of legislation, the enrolled bill, is sent to the president.

Resources:
- THOMAS, <*http://thomas.loc.gov*>
- GPO Access, <*www.gpoaccess.gov/bills/*>

Legislation is signed into law by the president.

The White House sends the signed copy to the National Archives, Office of the Federal Register (OFR). The National Archives assigns a public law number and the Government Printing Office (GPO) prints the bill as a public law, or "slip law."

Resources:
- National Archives, OFR, <*www.archives.gov/federal-register/laws/*>
- GPO Access, <*www.gpoaccess.gov/plaws/*>

Public laws are compiled chronologically for *Statutes At Large* volumes.

The annual volumes are compiled by the OFR and printed by GPO. The full set of volumes is not available on a free web site, although GPO has begun to publish an electronic version at <*www.gpoaccess. gov/statutes/*>. The printed volumes are available for sale by GPO or can be used at a local GPO Federal Depository Library.

Resources:
- GPO Online Bookstore, <*http://bookstore.gpo.gov*>
- GPO Federal Depository Library Directory, <*www.gpoaccess.gov/libraries.html*>

(Laws are also compiled in the commercially published *United States Code Congressional and Administrative News* from Thomson-West, <*http://west.thomson.com*>.)

Public laws of a "general and permanent" nature are compiled by topic for the United States Code.

The Law Revision Counsel of the House of Representatives assigns law text to the Code's topical hierarchy. The official *U.S. Code* is published

(continued on page 43)

§3.60 From Bills to Laws: Documents and Information Resources (continued)

by GPO every six years, within interim supplements. Many researchers prefer to use unofficial versions that are published commercially on such for-fee online services as Westlaw, *<http://west.thomson.com/store/>,* or free services such as Cornell University's Legal Information Institute.

Resources:

- House Law Revision Counsel, *<http://uscode.house.gov/>*
- GPO Access, *<www.gpoaccess.gov/uscode/>*
- Cornell Legal Information Institute, *<www.law.cornell.edu/uscode/>*

(The Code is also published commercially as the *United States Code Annotated*, from Thomson-West, *<http://west.thomson.com>*, and the *United States Code Service*, from LexisNexis, *<www.lexisnexis.com>*).

The United States Code is continually amended as new bills are signed into law.

<www.gpoaccess.gov> addresses will be transitioning to FDsys, *<www.fdsys.gov>* throughout 2009.

of the past month. Subscribers can also choose to receive alerts only when the content is related to a selected topic, such as homeland security or veterans' affairs. GAO offers an RSS feed as well.

Commercial Sources (paid subscription services)

- CQ.com, *<www.cq.com>*, provides alert services with legislative news, analysis, and documents.

- GalleryWatch.com, *<www.gallerywatch.com>*, has a Legislative Tracking and Notification Service.

- LexisNexis, *<www.lexisnexis.com>*, and Westlaw, *<http://west. thomson.com>*, each carry legislative databases such as the *Congressional Record*, and each offer alert services.

Unofficial Sources (free)

- GovTrack.us, *<www.govtrack.com>*, is a free database of federal legislative information. It provides email and RSS feed "trackers," alerts to new legislative actions. GovTrack is maintained by web developer Joshua Tauberer.

- OpenCongress, *<www.opencongress.org>*, provides numerous RSS feeds reporting on legislation. For a list of what is available, see *<www.opencongress.org/about/rss>*. OpenCongress is a joint project of the Sunlight Foundation and the Participatory Politics Foundation.

§3.70 United States Code Titles

"The United States Code (USC) is the codification by subject matter of the general and permanent laws of the United States. It is divided by broad subjects into 50 titles and published by the Office of the Law Revision Counsel of the U.S. House of Representatives. Since 1926, the United States Code has been published every six years. In between editions, annual cumulative supplements are published in order to present the most current information."

—Government Printing Office, *<www.gpoaccess.gov/uscode/>*

USC Titles

Title 1	General Provisions
Title 2	The Congress
Title 3	The President
Title 4	Flag and Seal, Seat of Government, and the States
Title 5	Government Organization and Employees; and Appendix
Title 6	Domestic Security
Title 7	Agriculture
Title 8	Aliens and Nationality
Title 9	Arbitration
Title 10	Armed Forces; and Appendix
Title 11	Bankruptcy; and Appendix
Title 12	Banks and Banking
Title 13	Census
Title 14	Coast Guard
Title 15	Commerce and Trade
Title 16	Conservation
Title 17	Copyrights

(continued on page 45)

USC Titles (continued)

Title 18	Crimes and Criminal Procedure; and Appendix
Title 19	Customs Duties
Title 20	Education
Title 21	Food and Drugs
Title 22	Foreign Relations and Intercourse
Title 23	Highways
Title 24	Hospitals and Asylums
Title 25	Indians
Title 26	Internal Revenue Code; and Appendix
Title 27	Intoxicating Liquors
Title 28	Judiciary and Judicial Procedure; and Appendix
Title 29	Labor
Title 30	Mineral Lands and Mining
Title 31	Money and Finance
Title 32	National Guard
Title 33	Navigation and Navigable Waters
Title 34	Navy (Repealed)
Title 35	Patents
Title 36	Patriotic Societies and Observances
Title 37	Pay and Allowances of the Uniformed Services
Title 38	Veterans' Benefits; and Appendix
Title 39	Postal Service
Title 40	Public Buildings, Property, and Works; and Appendix
Title 41	Public Contracts
Title 42	The Public Health and Welfare
Title 43	Public Lands
Title 44	Public Printing and Documents
Title 45	Railroads
Title 46	Shipping; and Appendix
Title 47	Telegraphs, Telephones, and Radiotelegraphs
Title 48	Territories and Insular Possessions
Title 49	Transportation
Title 50	War and National Defense; and Appendix

The *United States Code* is available online for free at several web sites, including:

- House Law Revision Counsel, *<http://uscode.house.gov/>*

- GPO Access, at *<www.gpoaccess.gov/uscode/>*

- Cornell's Legal Information Institute, at *<www.law.cornell.edu/uscode/>*

§3.80 Additional Legislative Branch Sources

§3.81 Congressional Research Service Reports

The Congressional Research Service, *<www.loc.gov/crsinfo/>*, a nonpartisan congressional support agency located within the Library of Congress, provides Congress with independent policy research and analysis. CRS prepares reports exclusively for Congress. CRS reports are not distributed directly to the public, although the public can request copies from their elected representatives in Congress.

Because CRS policy papers are not freely and directly available to the public, various for-profit and nonprofit organizations have developed services to obtain and distribute them. The web site Open CRS, *<http://open crs.com>*, from the nonprofit organization, Center for Democracy & Technology, *<www.cdt.org>*, provides free, one-stop access to many of the CRS reports that have become publicly available, but it is not a complete collection. Other organizations providing free access to partial collections of CRS reports include:

- Federation of American Scientists, *<www.fas.org/sgp/crs/>*

- National Agricultural Law Center, *<www.nationalaglawcenter.org/crs/>*

- State Department Foreign Press Center, *<http://fpc.state.gov/c18185.htm>*

- University of Maryland School of Law, *<www.law.umaryland.edu/marshall/crsreports/>*

In many cases, CRS may have issued a newer version of a report than is available from these sites. Your representatives in Congress can provide current copies upon request.

GalleryWatch, *<www.gallerywatch.com>*, a commercial, for-fee online service, has a searchable database of CRS reports.

Some CRS reports can also be found via Google or other Internet search engines if you know the title, author, or report number.

§3.82 Lobbyist Registrations

The House and Senate each have portal pages for finding the lobby disclosure reports filed with each chamber and for information about the disclosure requirements. The shortcut web address for the Senate's disclosure portal is *<www.senate.gov/lobby>*. The Clerk of the House maintains a portal for House filings and other disclosure information at *<http://lobbyingdisclosure.house.gov/>*.

§3.99 Chapter Summary and Review Questions

Chapter Summary

An understanding of the legislative process and familiarity with congressional documents is fundamental to legislative research. The core free, public web sites for legislative research are the House and Senate web sites, THOMAS from the Library of Congress, and GPO Access (to be replaced by the end of 2009 with new system called FDsys).

Review Questions

- What is the name for the version of a bill that is approved by both chambers of Congress and sent to the President?
- Name several resources you could use to follow floor activity in the House and Senate.
- What is the United States Code and where can you find it online?

Chapter Four

Judicial Branch Research

Legal research is a specialized practice that involves an understanding of the area of law being researched as well as the tools being used. Advanced legal research often requires the use of commercial online services such as the law firm standards LexisNexis (commonly misspelled "LexusNexus"), <*www.lexisnexis.com*>, and Westlaw, <*http://west.thomson.com/*>, or other paid-subscription resources such as Loislaw.com and Versuslaw.com. For the limited research that those outside the legal professions may need to do, free web sites such as FindLaw.com and the various court and law library web sites may suffice.

TheCapitol.Net also has a page of links to legal resources, "Legal Reference and Research Tools," at <*www.thecapitol.net/Research/legalFTL.htm*>.

This section provides basic information on the federal courts, judiciary, and useful web sites for non-specialists.

§4.0 Federal Court System Structure

Supreme Court	United States Supreme Court (commonly abbreviated as SCOTUS) <*www.supremecourtus.gov*>
Appellate courts	United States Courts of Appeal <*www.uscourts.gov/courtlinks*> —Includes twelve regional courts of appeal and the Court of Appeals for the Federal Circuit
Trial courts	United States District Courts <*www.uscourts.gov/courtlinks*> —Includes ninety-four judicial districts and the United States Bankruptcy Courts Court of International Trade <*www.cit.uscourts.gov*> Court of Federal Claims <*www.uscfc.uscourts.gov*>
Other federal tribunals that are not within the judicial branch	Military courts (trial and appellate) United States Court of Appeals for Veterans Claims <*www.vetapp.gov*> United States Tax Court <*www.ustaxcourt.gov*> Administrative agency offices and boards (A useful list of links is compiled by the University of Virginia Library at <*http://www2.lib.virginia.edu/govtinfo/ fed_decisions_agency.html*>.)

§4.10 Regional Federal Court Circuits —Geographic Coverage

(All federal circuit court web addresses are at <www.uscourts.gov/courtlinks>.)

Circuit	Geographic Coverage
First	Maine, Massachusetts, New Hampshire, Puerto Rico, Rhode Island
Second	Connecticut, New York, Vermont
Third	Delaware, New Jersey, Pennsylvania, U.S. Virgin Islands
Fourth	Maryland, North Carolina, South Carolina, Virginia, West Virginia
Fifth	Louisiana, Mississippi, Texas
Sixth	Kentucky, Michigan, Ohio, Tennessee
Seventh	Illinois, Indiana, Wisconsin
Eighth	Arkansas, Iowa, Minnesota, Missouri, Nebraska, North Dakota, South Dakota
Ninth	Alaska, Arizona, California, Guam, Hawaii, Idaho, Montana, Nevada, Northern Mariana Islands, Oregon, Washington
Tenth	Colorado, Kansas, New Mexico, Oklahoma, Utah, Wyoming
Eleventh	Alabama, Florida, Georgia
District of Columbia Circuit	Washington, DC
Federal Circuit	National jurisdiction. Hears appeals in specialized cases, such as those involving patent laws and cases decided by the Court of International Trade and the Court of Federal Claims.

§4.20 Sources of Supreme Court Opinions Online

Supreme Court of the United States

<www.supremecourtus.gov>

The Supreme Court's web site is the official online source for the Court's slip opinions. Opinions are available online for 2001 to present. Current opinions are posted to the web site in PDF format within hours after they are issued. Researchers can select an opinion from lists of opinions in date order. There is no word-search capability.

The Supreme Court site also has transcripts of *oral arguments* before the Court for the 2000 term to the present, with about a two-week delay.

FindLaw: Cases and Codes: Supreme Court Opinions

<www.findlaw.com/casecode/supreme.html>

FindLaw is a web site owned by the West Group, which also owns the Westlaw online information service. FindLaw has a free, searchable data-base of all Supreme Court opinions since 1893. (The Court issued its first opinion in 1792.) Opinions on FindLaw can be searched by word, party name, and *U.S. Reports* citation[1].

FindLaw also has a section called Supreme Court Center. Among other resources, it includes copies of *legal briefs* filed in U.S. Supreme Court cases from 1999 to present and a subject index to opinions from the current term. FindLaw's Supreme Court Center is at *<http://supreme.lp.findlaw.com/supreme_court/resources.html>*.

Legal Information Institute Supreme Court Collection

<www.law.cornell.edu/supct/>

Cornell University's online Legal Information Institute service has the searchable text of Supreme Court decisions from 1990 to present. In addition, it features a collection of over 600 important *historic decisions* from the Court's more than 200-year history. Under the heading Archive of Decisions, the opinions are sorted by topic, author, and party name.

---

1. Supreme Court opinions are cited by the volume and page number of the official *United States Reports* volume in which they appear; for example: 347 U.S. 483.

Comparison of Supreme Court Opinion Sites

Web Site	Date Coverage	Word Search	Browse	Citation Search	Format(s)
Supreme Court <www.supreme courtus.gov>	2005 to present	No	Yes	No	PDF
FindLaw <www.findlaw. com/casecode/ supreme.html>	1893 to present	Yes	Yes	Yes	HTML
Legal Information Institute <www.law.cornell. edu/supct/>	1990 to present + historical selection	Yes	Yes	No	HTML PDF

§4.30 The Federal Courts: Selected Internet Resources

Courts and Opinions

- Administrative Office of the U.S. Courts
  <*www.uscourts.gov*>
  Links to all federal court sites and to educational information on the federal judiciary.

- Federal Law Materials—Judicial Opinions
  <*www.law.cornell.edu/federal/opinions.html*>
  Links and coverage notes for free, public web sites carrying federal judicial opinions.

- Georgetown Law Library Research Guides
  <*www.ll.georgetown.edu/research/*>
  Guides to the key books, databases, and web sites for a wide variety of legal topics.

§4.31 Low-Cost Legal Research Sources

Georgetown University's Edward Bennett Williams Law Library maintains a useful online guide called "Free & Low Cost Legal Research," *<www.ll.georgetown.edu/guides/freelowcost.cfm>*. The guide covers U.S. federal legal information. It links to selected legal research resources. For the less expensive legal database services, the guide identifies their features, costs, and limits.

- PACER (Public Access to Court Electronic Records)
  <http://pacer.psc.uscourts.gov>
  Centralized system run by the Administrative Office of the U.S. Courts for access to court case dockets from U.S. district, bankruptcy, and appellate courts and a national party/case index for those courts. PACER charges modest fees, and users must register for an account.

- Public Library of Law
  <www.plol.org>
  Free access to U.S. federal case law and other legal documents, operated by Fastcase.com, Inc. The Public Library of Law is one of several fairly new web sites offering free access to case law; others include: AltLaw, *<http://altlaw.org>*, and Justia, *<http://law.justia.com/us/>*.

Federal Judges

- Federal Judicial Vacancies
  <www.uscourts.gov/judicialvac.html>
  The Federal Judicial Conference tracks statistics on vacancies, nominations, and confirmations at this site.

- Judges of the United States Courts
  <www.fjc.gov/history/home.nsf>
  Biographies of federal judges from 1789 to present.

§4.40 Citing the Law

Legal professionals adhere to a standard style for citing legal and other information resources so the material can easily be found by others. Citations usually indicate the name of the legal source (abbreviated), the volume and page number(s), and date. For example, an opinion of the Supreme Court would be cited as *New York v. Quarles*, 467 U.S. 649 (1984). If a particular statement within the opinion is being cited, the citation would also include the official page number where that statement can be found, such as 467 U.S. 649, 655. Electronic sources often include the official pagination so that individual pages can be cited even if the document is not in book form.

A good basic guide is available online. "Introduction to Basic Legal Citation," by Peter W. Martin, can be consulted or downloaded in whole at *<www.law.cornell.edu/citation/index.htm>*. The guide includes examples for electronic resources, judicial opinions, public laws, regulations, and other document types.

The standard reference for legal citation is a book commonly referred to as "The Bluebook." The book, *The Bluebook: A Uniform System of Citation* (Cambridge, MA: The Harvard Law Review Association), is available online from the publisher's web address, *<www.legalbluebook.com>*, for a subscription fee. It can also be found in print at many bookstores and libraries.

§4.41 Citing Decisions at the Federal Level— Examples

Supreme Court:	*Brown v. Board of Education*, 347 U.S. 483 (1954)
Courts of Appeal:	*Reed v. Sullivan*, 988 F.2d 812, 816 (8th Cir. 1993)
	Culbertson v. Shalala, 30 F.3d 934 (8th Cir. 1994)
District Courts:	*Padilla v. Bush*, 233 F. Supp. 2d 564 (S.D.N.Y. 2002)
	South Dakota v. Adams, 506 F. Supp. 50 (D.S.D. 1980)

§4.50 Law Dictionaries

The practice of law requires a specialized vocabulary. Several free, online dictionaries can help.

- FindLaw Law Dictionary, *<http://dictionary.lp.findlaw.com>*.
- Nolo's Legal Glossary, *<www.nolo.com/glossary.cfm>*

§4.99 Chapter Summary and Review Questions

Chapter Summary

Professional legal research requires knowledge of the area of law being researched and often requires access to and skill with commercial search services. For non-lawyers, a variety of free web sites facilitate the retrieval of legal documents.

Review Questions

- What is the basic structure of the U.S. federal court system?
- Where can you find direct links to federal court web sites?
- How would you use this citation to find the court case it cites?
  468 U.S. 364 (1984)

Chapter Five

Executive Branch Research

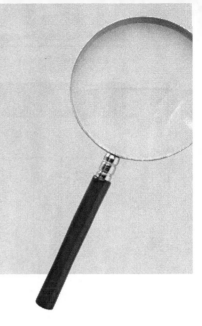

The executive branch includes the Executive Office of the President, fifteen departments, and numerous independent agencies, commissions, boards, and other entities. The official U.S. government web site, USA.gov (*<www.usa.gov>*), provides central access to the web resources of the executive branch, and also links to legislative and judicial branch sites.

This section includes information on using USA.gov and on finding the regulatory, administrative, and other resources of the executive branch.

RealWorldResearchSkills.com

§5.0 Executive Branch Organization

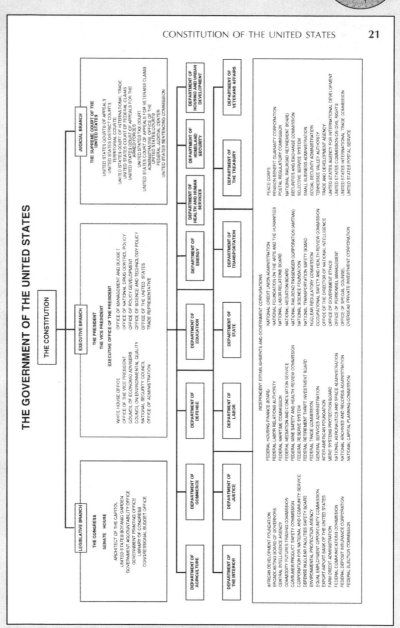

CONSTITUTION OF THE UNITED STATES 21

THE GOVERNMENT OF THE UNITED STATES

Source: The United States Government Manual, 2008-2009, <www.gpoaccess.gov/gmanual>

§5.10 USA.gov
<www.usa.gov>

Scope:
- Links to federal, state, local, and tribal government web sites and to nongovernment sites with government-related information.
- Search engine for federal and state government information on the web.
- Special sections for citizens, businesses and nonprofits, federal employees, and governments.
- Spanish-language version, linked from USA.gov home page.

Sponsor:
General Services Administration, on behalf of the White House and executive branch.

Description:
USA.gov describes itself as "the U.S. Government's Official Web Portal." The site is an interagency initiative managed by the General Services Administration to provide organized access to U.S. government information.

USA.gov organizes links to government information by topic, audience, agency, and other schemes. The USA.gov search engine is a key feature.

This site is useful for finding government information when you do not know which agency will have it and for locating the URLs for government web sites.

USA.gov Search Engine Tips:
A **basic search** box is in the upper right corner of the home page. This searches the content on the USA.gov site and on many other government web sites. To search:
- Enter your search words.
- Review results, which are displayed in relevance-ranked order.

The **advanced search** screen allows you to set specific parameters to narrow your search. These include:
- Limiting to only English-language or only Spanish-language results.
- Limiting by file format, such as only PDF documents or only Microsoft PowerPoint files.

- Limiting your search to one, or several, specific government web sites.
- On the search results screen, use the Agencies tab to sort results by agency source. Use the All link to see the full Agencies sort.

No search engine is comprehensive. Try USA.gov along with alternatives, such as a relevant federal agency's web site or a general search engine.

Information for Researchers:

USA.gov has a number of sections to assist the Washington researcher. Most are grouped under Reference Center in the left-hand column. Click on "more" in this section to see the complete listing.

Highlights include:

- **Data and Statistics.** Links to the federal statistics gateway site, FedStats.gov, and to other federal statistical sites such as EconomicIndicators.gov and ChildStats.gov.

- **Graphics and Photos.** An index to government web pages that offer collections of graphics and photos, most of which can be downloaded. Most, but not all, government content is free of copyright restrictions. Review the disclaimer on USA.gov and at individual agency sites before downloading for re-use.

- **Laws and Regulations.** Links to federal and state web sites for laws, regulations, court directories, and related information. *(Tip: searchers may find nongovernment alternatives, such as Findlaw.com or the Legal Information Institute, at <www.law. cornell.edu>, to be more helpful.)*

- **News.** This section includes several useful links. "Federal Agency News and Press Releases" is an index to federal executive, legislative, and judicial branch web pages that include government news releases. The "Government Email Newsletters" page provides easy subscription access to a broad selection of free government email newsletters.

The "Phone" section under Contact Your Government, in the left-hand column of the USA.gov home page, is also useful for researchers. This section includes:

- **Federal Employee Phone Directories, by Agency.** Links to major government phone directories online, as well as to the individual agency phone directories online at agency sites.

§5.11 USA.gov Home Page

Source: <www.usa.gov>

§5.12 Government Search Engines

- **USASearch.gov**, *<http://usasearch.gov>*, links to the USA.gov search engine, which is also available on the USA.gov home page.

- **Google U.S. Government Search**, *<www.google.com/unclesam>*, is an alternative to USASearch.gov. Like USASearch.gov, it has an advanced search.

- **DTIC Online**, *<www.dtic.mil>*, has a search box that, by default, searches "DoD Sites and Collections." The search includes the .mil domain plus military web sites like the National Defense University, *<www.ndu.edu>*, that are not in the .mil domain.

USA.gov Tips:

The USA.gov site links to both government and nongovernment web sites that cover government-related topics. Be aware that most links take you off the USA.gov site. Check the sponsor or author of the content for each new site you reach through USA.gov.

USA.gov is best used to discover which government web sites cover a topic. Once those sites have been found, you may wish to explore them directly to find newer or more relevant content.

§5.20 Sources for Presidential and Other White House Documents

§5.21 Presidential Documents on Government Web Sites

White House Web Site

<www.whitehouse.gov>

- White House blog
- President's weekly video address
- Press briefings and press releases
- Executive orders
- Presidential memoranda
- Presidential proclamations

National Archives

<www.archives.gov>

- Executive Order disposition tables, *<www.archives.gov/federal-register/executive-orders/disposition.html>*.

- Web sites for the libraries of former presidents, *<www.archives.gov/presidential-libraries/>*; includes guide to presidential documents online, *<www.archives.gov/presidential-libraries/research/guide.html>*.

GPO Access

<www.gpoaccess.gov/executive.html>

GPO FDsys

<www.fdsys.gov>

- Daily Compilation of Presidential Documents (January 20, 2009–)

- Weekly Compilation of Presidential Documents (1993–)

- Public Papers of the Presidents (1991–2004, as of early 2009)

- *Federal Register* (1995–current) and Title 3 of the *Code of Federal Regulations* for Executive Orders (1996–current)

 ## §5.22 Presidential Documents on Nongovernment Web Sites

The American Presidency Project

<www.presidency.ucsb.edu>

- This project is building an extensive collection of current and historic documents. It includes the Public Papers of the President from 1929 forward and the State of the Union Addresses from 1790 forward. The site also has information on presidential elections.

Georgetown Law Library: Presidential Documents

<www.ll.georgetown.edu/guides/presidential_documents.cfm>

- This site provides information on print and online resources. Note that it is tailored for students using the Georgetown University Law Library.

§5.23 President's Budget Documents

The principal volumes that are usually part of the president's annual budget submission include the following:

- **Budget** (officially the *Budget of the United States Government*)— includes the president's budget message, presentations on the president's major budgetary initiatives organized by department and major agencies (or, in some years, by budget function), discussions of management initiatives and performance data, and summary tables.

- **Appendix**—sets forth detailed information for accounts within each department and agency, including funding levels, program descriptions, proposed appropriations language, and object classification and employment data.

- **Analytical Perspectives**—contains analyses and information on specific aspects of the budget or budget-related areas, such as budget and performance integration, economic assumptions, and current services estimates; crosscutting programs, such as research and development, federal investment and aid to state and local governments; and budget process reform proposals.

- **Historical Tables**—provides data, covering an extended time period, on receipts, budget authority, outlays, deficits and surpluses, federal debt, and other matters.

Within a few days of the submission of the budget, the president also transmits an annual ***Economic Report of the President*** to Congress, which includes the report of the Council of Economic Advisers.

The president is required by law to update his submissions, and he does this in a far briefer, more summary fashion in his ***Midsession Review***, which is due by July 15.

Online access to the president's budget documents is available in several places, including the Office of Management and Budget web site, *<www.whitehouse.gov/omb/>*, and GPO FDsys, *<www.fdsys.gov>*.

Source: § 9.43, *Congressional Deskbook, <CongressionalDeskbook.com>*

Presidential Directives and Executive Orders

<www.fas.org/irp/offdocs/direct.htm>

- The Federation of American Scientists (FAS) web site provides the text of the presidential decision directives from the year 1947 forward that FAS has been able to obtain.

§5.24 Office of Management and Budget Documents

The Office of Management and Budget (OMB) coordinates preparation of the president's budget, plays a leading role in its defense in Congress, and oversees implementation of the spending bills passed by Congress. OMB policies take many forms. The following types of publications contain instructions and guidelines to other federal entities from OMB:

- **Circulars**, expected to have a continuing effect of generally two years or more.

- **Bulletins**, containing guidance of a more transitory nature that would normally expire after one or two years.

- **Regulations** and **Paperwork**, daily reports that list regulations and paperwork under OMB review.

- **Financial Management** policies and **Grants Management** circulars and related documents.

- **Federal Register** submissions, including copies of proposed and final rules.

For information on OMB policies and publications, check the OMB web site (<*www.whitehouse.gov/omb/*>) and the Federal Register (at GPO FDsys, <*www.fdsys.gov*>).

Source: § 9.42, *Congressional Deskbook*, <*CongressionalDeskbook.com*>

§5.30 Agency Web Site Content

Federal department and agency web sites contain a wide array of information. Content varies from agency to agency, but federal agency web sites often include:

- Agency contact information
- Agency leadership biographies and speeches
- Annual reports and strategic plans
- Budget documents
- Congressional testimony from agency officials
- Databases and publications related to the regulatory, research, education, or outreach mission of the agency
- Educational materials for students and teachers

- Freedom of Information Act (FOIA) instructions
- Inspector General reports
- Laws and regulations under which the agency operates or which they are responsible for enforcing
- Legal or administrative decisions, orders, or guidance issued by the agency
- Links to the agency's presence on third party sites such as Twitter, Facebook, and YouTube.
- News releases and media kits
- Organization charts
- Procurement, grants, or technology transfer opportunities

§5.40 Federal Regulations

For an overview of the federal regulatory process, see the Federal Regulatory Process Poster, by Ken Ackerman, ISBN 1-58733-013-X, TheCapitol. Net, 2006, *<www.thecapitol.net/Publications/agencyposter.htm>*.

§5.41 Federal Register

Published by the Office of the Federal Register, National Archives and Records Administration (NARA), the *Federal Register* is the official daily publication for rules, proposed rules, and notices of federal agencies, as well as executive orders and other presidential documents.

Federal Register

<www.fdsys.gov/fdsys/browse/collection.action?collectionCode=FR>

Search or browse the full text of the *Federal Register*, from 1994 to present. Documents are available in HTML and PDF formats for 2000 to present, in plain text and PDF for 1995–2000, and in plain text only for 1994.

Federal Register— Documents on Public Inspection

<www.federalregister.gov/inspection.aspx>

The National Archives' Electronic Public Inspection Desk carries documents that will appear in the next day's *Federal Register* and selected documents scheduled for later issues.

§5.42 Overview of the Rulemaking Process

1. Grant of rulemaking authority

- Congress delegates authority directly to agencies
- President may delegate constitutional authority to subordinates
- President or agency head may re-delegate authority to subordinates

2. Proposed Rule stage

- Office of Management and Budget (OMB) reviews under E.O. 12866
- Agencies publish Proposed Rule in *Federal Register* (FR) for public comment

3. Final Rule stage

- OMB reviews again under E.O. 12866
- Agencies publish final rule in FR
  - respond to comments, amend *Code of Federal Regulations*, set effective date

4. Congressional review

- Agencies submit rules to Congress and Government Accountability Office (could nullify rule)

5. Effective date

- Thirty-day minimum, sixty days for major rule, no minimum for good cause
- Agency may delay or withdraw rule before it becomes effective

Federal Register Tutorial

<www.archives.gov/federal-register/tutorial/index.html>

This tutorial can be viewed online in HTML or PDF format, or downloaded in its entirety. It explains the regulatory process, the *Federal Register*, and the *Code of Federal Regulations*. The tutorial page also links to guides on drafting documents for publication in the *Federal Register*.

§5.43 GPO FDsys: Federal Register
<www.fdsys.gov/fdsys/browse/collection.action?
collectionCode=FR>

Scope:

- Issues of the *Federal Register* published from 1994 to the current issue.

Sponsor:

Government Printing Office. (Content is provided by the Office of the Federal Register, National Archives and Records Administration.)

Description:

FDsys contains *Federal Register* volumes from 59 (1994) to the present. Documents are available in Summary, PDF, ASCII text, or HTML format. HTML documents are available from 2000 forward and provide hypertext links to Web sites mentioned in the *Federal Register* document.

Items in the *Federal Register* are cited by volume and page number, with year; for example:

69 Fed. Reg. 29171 (2004)

Search Tips:

Searching *Federal Register* by Agency

Examples:

Using the Simple Search Box, enter

collection:fr agency:"health and human services"

Using the Advanced Search page,

1) Select *Federal Register* from Available Collections

2) Click Add to add *Federal Register* to the Selected Collections box

3) Select Agency under Search in

4) Enter health and human services in the textbox marked **for**

Searching *Federal Register* by Citation (Volume and Page Number)

Examples:

Using the Simple Search Box, enter

collection:fr citation:"71 fr 43345"

Using the Advanced Search page,

1) Select *Federal Register* from Available Collections

2) Click Add to add *Federal Register* to the Selected Collections box

3) Select Citation from Search in

4) Enter "71 fr 43345" in the textbox marked **for**

§5.44 Code of Federal Regulations

The *Code of Federal Regulations* (CFR) is the codification of the general and permanent rules published in the *Federal Register* by the executive departments and agencies of the federal government. It is divided into fifty titles that represent broad areas subject to federal regulation. Each volume of the CFR is updated once each calendar year.

Code of Federal Regulations

<www.gpoaccess.gov/cfr/>

Search the CFR by word, retrieve CFR sections by citation, or browse by CFR title and part. Documents are in PDF and plain text formats. Editions of CFR titles are online for 1997 through the present; some 1996 titles are also available. The CFR will be available on the new GPO FDsys system in 2009.

List of CFR Sections Affected

<www.gpoaccess.gov/lsa/>

The *List of CFR Sections Affected* (LSA) lists proposed, new, and amended federal regulations published in the *Federal Register* since the most recent revision date of a CFR title. The LSA will be available on the new GPO FDsys system in 2009.

§5.45 GPO Access: Code of Federal Regulations
<www.gpoaccess.gov/cfr/>

Scope:
- Current text of the *Code of Federal Regulations* (*CFR*).
- Text of previous editions of the *CFR*, going back to 1996 or 1997, depending on title.
- The CFR will become available on GPO FDsys (*<www.fdsys.gov>*) in 2009. When it becomes available, the FDsys help section will provide CFR search tips.

Sponsor:
Government Printing Office. (Content is provided by the Office of the Federal Register, National Archives and Records Administration.)

Description:
The CFR organizes the general and permanent regulations of executive branch departments and agencies into fifty broad subject areas, or titles, such as Energy, Internal Revenue, and Public Health. Each title is updated once each calendar year with the regulations issued in the *Federal Register* throughout the previous year: titles 1–16 are updated as of January 1; titles 17–27 as of April 1; titles 28–41 as of July 1; and titles 42–50 as of October 1.

Items in the CFR are typically cited by title and section, with year; for example:

34 C.F.R. § 1100.2 (2003)

GPO Access allows users to search the CFR by word, retrieve CFR sections by citation, or browse by CFR title and part.

Search Tips:
- Word searching works the same as in the *Federal Register* on GPO Access.
- To retrieve a known CFR citation, search for it in any of the following ways:
  - in the word search box in quotes, in this example format: "34CFR1100.2";

– with the Retrieve by CFR Citation fill-in search form; or

– with the Browse feature to select title, then part, then section.

- For a more precise search, use the Browse and/or Search feature and select a specific CFR title or titles to search within.

Updating the CFR:

CFR titles are only updated annually. A number of tools exist to help you learn if a CFR section has been changed by any new regulations since the CFR title was last updated. Options include:

- Searching the *Federal Register* for the time period since your CFR title was last updated.

- Using the *List of Sections Affected* on GPO Access. Note: Although GPO Access includes instructions, this can be a tedious and confusing process.

- Using the GPO Access service called e-CFR (see page 64).

§5.46 Code of Federal Regulations Titles

"The Code of Federal Regulations (CFR) is an annual codification of the general and permanent rules published in the *Federal Register* by the executive departments and agencies of the Federal Government.

"The CFR is divided into 50 titles representing broad areas subject to Federal regulation.

"Each Title is divided into chapters that are assigned to agencies issuing regulations pertaining to that broad subject area. Each chapter is divided into parts and each part is then divided into sections—the basic unit of the CFR.

"The purpose of the CFR is to present the official and complete text of agency regulations in one organized publication and to provide a comprehensive and convenient reference for all those who may need to know the text of general and permanent Federal regulations."

—The National Archives and Records Administration

<www.archives.gov/federal-register/cfr/about.html>

§5.47 CFR Titles

Title 1	General Provisions
Title 2	[Reserved]
Title 3	The President
Title 4	Accounts
Title 5	Administrative Personnel
Title 6	Homeland Security
Title 7	Agriculture
Title 8	Aliens and Nationality
Title 9	Animals and Animal Products
Title 10	Energy
Title 11	Federal Elections
Title 12	Banks and Banking
Title 13	Business Credit and Assistance
Title 14	Aeronautics and Space
Title 15	Commerce and Foreign Trade
Title 16	Commercial Practices
Title 17	Commodity and Securities Exchanges
Title 18	Conservation of Power and Water Resources
Title 19	Customs Duties
Title 20	Employees' Benefits
Title 21	Food and Drugs
Title 22	Foreign Relations
Title 23	Highways
Title 24	Housing and Urban Development
Title 25	Indians
Title 26	Internal Revenue
Title 27	Alcohol, Tobacco Products, and Firearms
Title 28	Judicial Administration
Title 29	Labor
Title 30	Mineral Resources

(continued on page 73)

§5.47 CFR Titles (continued)

Title 31	Money and Finance: Treasury
Title 32	National Defense
Title 33	Navigation and Navigable Waters
Title 34	Education
Title 35	Panama Canal
Title 36	Parks, Forests, and Public Property
Title 37	Patents, Trademarks, and Copyrights
Title 38	Pensions, Bonuses, and Veterans' Relief
Title 39	Postal Service
Title 40	Protection of Environment
Title 41	Public Contracts and Property Management
Title 42	Public Health
Title 43	Public Lands: Interior
Title 44	Emergency Management and Assistance
Title 45	Public Welfare
Title 46	Shipping
Title 47	Telecommunication
Title 48	Federal Acquisition Regulations System
Title 49	Transportation
Title 50	Wildlife and Fisheries

§5.48 Additional Regulatory Research Sources

Resources Covering All Agencies

OMB Office of Information and Regulatory Affairs (OIRA)—Regulatory Matters

<www.whitehouse.gov/omb/inforeg_regmatters/>

Includes the administration's regulatory policy and guidance documents. Links to RegInfo.gov, *<www.reginfo.gov>*, for information on regulations under OMB review.

RegInfo.gov

<www.reginfo.gov>

Portal to federal regulatory documents and information, maintained by the General Services Administration and OMB. Content includes *The Regulatory Plan and Unified Agenda of Federal Regulatory and Deregulatory Actions* and RegMap, a graphical overview of the rule-making process.

Regulations.gov

<www.regulations.gov>

A central database of proposed federal regulations and related documents with a feature for electronically filing comments on proposed regulations. Offers RSS feeds and email alerts for notification of new documents.

The Regulatory Plan and Unified Agenda of Federal Regulatory and Deregulatory Actions

<www.reginfo.gov/public/do/eAgendaMain>

The *Unified Agenda* is issued each spring as notice of specific regulatory changes under consideration by executive branch departments and agencies. The *Regulatory Plan*, published each year as the fall issue of the *Unified Agenda*, identifies the regulatory priorities of the departments and agencies.

Agency Tools—Selected Examples

Small Business Administration Regulatory Alerts

<www.sba.gov/advo/laws/law_regalerts.html>

Lists documents published in the *Federal Register* and open for comment that may significantly affect small businesses. The alerts are issued by SBA's Office of Advocacy.

EPA—Federal Register Environmental Documents

<www.epa.gov/fedrgstr/>

Includes past EPA documents published in the *Federal Register* and an option to receive notices of new EPA *Federal Register* documents via email. Also features EPA's regulatory agenda.

USDA—Food Safety & Inspection Service (FSIS)—Regulations & Policies

<www.fsis.usda.gov/regulations/>

Includes the regulatory agenda and FSIS documents published in the *Federal Register.*

Finding Aids and Guides

Georgetown University Law Library: Administrative Law Research Tutorial

<www.ll.georgetown.edu/tutorials/admin/index.html>

Covers agency regulations and decisions. Written for GU law students, but of use to all.

OMB Watch Regulatory Resource Center

<www.ombwatch.org/regresources>

Detailed information on tracking the regulations and understanding the federal rule-making process.

Regulatory Process Poster

<www.RegulatoryProcess.com>

A poster from TheCapitol.Net that outlines the federal regulatory process.

University of Virginia Library: Administrative Decisions & Other Actions

<www.lib.virginia.edu/govdocs/fed_decisions_agency.html>

Links to resources for administrative actions which are outside the scope of the *Code of Federal Regulations* or the *Federal Register*; for example, Revenue Rulings from the Internal Revenue Service and Directives from the Occupational Safety and Health Administration.

§5.50 Freedom of Information Act (FOIA)

The Freedom of Information Act (5 U.S.C. § 552) establishes the rules under which individuals can request and obtain access to unpublished records of federal executive branch agencies. Certain types of records—such as classified documents or those that would disclose confidential business information—are exempt from FOIA. In addition, FOIA does not apply to the federal judiciary or elected officials, including the president, vice president, and members of Congress. The requesting individual may have to pay a fee for the reproduction of the documents, and the processing time for FOIA requests can be lengthy.

Despite its limitations, many Washington researchers use FOIA as part of their information-gathering process. Some organizations routinely use FOIA to obtain documents and make them publicly available. As an example, see the National Security Archive at *<www.gwu.edu/~nsarchiv/>*.

 ## §5.51 Resources for Learning about and Using FOIA

Most federal agencies have a link to FOIA information on their web sites.

"Effective FOIA Requesting for Everyone"

<www.gwu.edu/~nsarchiv/nsa/foia/foia_guide.html>

This guide to FOIA and other methods for obtaining federal agency documents was written by FOIA experts at the National Security Archive (NSA). The NSA also provides a step-by-step chart of the FOIA process, *<www.gwu.edu/~nsarchiv/nsa/foia/foia_flowchart.pdf>*.

Principal FOIA Contacts at Federal Agencies

<www.justice.gov/04foia/foiacontacts.htm>

This online directory from the Justice Department links to the FOIA web pages at federal agency web sites. It also provides names, addresses, and phone numbers for the agencies' FOIA contacts.

FOIA Reference Materials

<www.usdoj.gov/04foia/04_7.html>

The Justice Department links to a number of useful documents and guides on this page, including the *FOIA Post* newsletter and the text of the Freedom of Information Act.

Media Relations Handbook, by Brad Fitch (TheCapitol.Net 2004)

<MediaRelationsHandbook.com>

Appendix 4, "Your Right to Federal Records: Questions and Answers on the Freedom of Information Act and Privacy Act."

"Your Right to Federal Records: Questions and Answers on the Freedom of Information Act and Privacy Act"

<www.pueblo.gsa.gov/cic_text/fed_prog/foia/foia.htm>

The General Services Administration Federal Citizen Information Center provides this guide for citizens who wish to use the Freedom of Information Act.

 ## §5.60 Federal Regulatory Agencies: Filings Databases

Federal laws and regulations require certain individuals, companies, organizations, and other entities to file information with a government agency. This information is often available to the public via the Internet, although in some cases researchers must still go to public records rooms in Washington to retrieve documents.

The following list highlights some of the government filings databases available on the web. In some cases, a nongovernmental organization provides its own interface to the same government information; several such examples are noted in the entries below.

FCC Radio and Television Station Filings (page titled "CDBS Public Access")

<http://svartifoss2.fcc.gov/prod/cdbs/pubacc/prod/cdbs_pa.htm>

The Media Bureau of the Federal Communications Commission (FCC) regulates radio and television broadcasting. Their filings databases provide information on station ownership, mailing addresses, and other matters.

FEC Campaign Filings Reports and Data (page titled "Campaign Finance Reports and Data")

<www.fec.gov/disclosure.shtml>

The Federal Election Commission (FEC) has financial filings from federal candidates, campaign committees, political parties, and political action committees. Several nongovernmental organizations make the same filings available online with additional search features or data compilations; a popular example is Opensecrets.org (*<www.opensecrets.org>*) from the Center for Responsive Politics.

SEC IDEA

<www.sec.gov/idea/searchidea/webusers.htm>

The Securities and Exchange Commission's IDEA system makes public companies' SEC filings available online. SEC filings include information on finances, ownership, investors, executive compensation, and other matters. IDEA also provides mutual funds disclosures. IDEA is the replacement for the SEC's former database, EDGAR. One free alternative to the official SEC site is SEC Info, *<www.secinfo.com>*, by Fran Finnegan & Company. Several commercial online services provide fee-based access to the same filings, adding features such as better formatting of the corporate reports or more historical coverage.

§5.99 Chapter Summary and Review Questions

Chapter Summary

The official U.S. government web portal USA.gov and its search engine, USASearch.gov, help locate information on the vast federal government web. Government and nongovernment sites assist in locating presidential and regulatory documents. The Freedom of Information Act can be used to request documents not publicly available; learn about the process and its limitations before relying on FOIA.

Review Questions

- Name two specialized search engines for searching U.S. government information on the web.
- What type of information can you typically find on a government agency web site?
- What types of documents can you find in the Federal Register?
- Where can you get advance notice of documents scheduled to appear in tomorrow's Federal Register?

Chapter Six

State and International Research

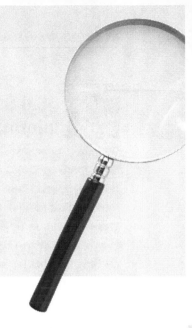

While this book focuses on national information resources, the Washington researcher often must consult state or international resources to track matters of interest. This section provides a brief introduction to some of the most helpful Internet resources for state and international research.

§6.0 State Government Information Resources

Washington researchers are often in need of state government information. State agencies may study an issue before or in more depth than the federal government does, particularly if the issue has significant local impact. State legislatures may draft laws on an issue before the U.S. Congress considers it. States may collect local statistics in more detail than is available at the national level. States are the primary sources of information on entities regulated at the state level: licensed business, registered voters, and motor vehicle drivers, for example. Also, states have a key role in many federal programs, such as transportation funding and Medicare.

State government professional organizations—for example, the National Governors Association, *<www.nga.org>*, or the National Association of Secretaries of State, *<www.nass.org>*—provide fifty-state directories and compilations that can be essential to your research. We mention several such groups in this chapter.

§6.1 Search State Government Sites

USAsearch.gov, *<www.usasearch.gov>*, is a search engine for U.S. federal, state, and local government web sites. Web sites for all levels of government are searched simultaneously, and there is no option to limit a search to just state or local sites. To find state and local results, use the Agencies tab to view results by source and use the All option to view all sources.

State Agency Databases, *<http://wikis.ala.org/godort/index.php/State_Agency_Databases>*, links to databases available on state web sites. As is the case with database information at the federal level, much of the information on state government databases cannot be searched directly using Google or other search engines. To address this problem, the American Libraries Association Government Documents group maintains this directory of many, *not all*, databases at the state government level. Coverage varies greatly from state to state, but typical databases provide access to economic information, attorney general opinions, unclaimed property lists, names of state-licensed professionals, and information on state-regulated entities.

§6.2 **State News and Statistics**

Stateline.org, *<www.stateline.org>*, reports on state government news and links to related articles in U.S. newspapers. News stories are arranged by issue area, such as education and health care. Links to major policy organizations are also arranged by issue area. Stateline.org is sponsored by the Pew Charitable Trusts.

State Capital Newspapers, *<www.ncsl.org/programs/press/dailynews/ cpapers.htm>*, links to newspapers covering state government news. The web page is part of the National Conference of State Legislatures site.

Statistics at the state level are available from many federal web sites and from the state web sites themselves. FedStats.gov, *<www.fedstats. gov>*, is a simple portal to federal statistics on the web. It includes Map-Stats, *<www.fedstats.gov/qf/>*, an interface to federal statistics at the state level. American FactFinder, *<http://factfinder.census.gov/>*, the Census Bureau's main data portal, also provides easy access to data at the state level.

§6.3 **Find State Government Information by Branch**

Each state government's main web site serves as a portal to its legislature, governor's office, agencies, and courts. State home page links are maintained at the USA.gov State Government web page, *<www.usa.gov/ Agencies/State_and_Territories.shtml>*. Many specialized web sites, particularly professional associations representing state officials, have compiled information for all fifty states.

§6.4 **State Legislative Branch Resources**

The National Council of State Legislatures, *<www.ncsl.org>*, supports its members, the state legislatures, with advocacy, research, and other services. Useful information on the NCSL web site includes state legislative elections data, policy statements, and compilations, including:

- State Legislature Internet Links, *<www.ncsl.org/public/leglinks.cfm>*, for direct links to state legislature web sites and specific site sections, such as legislative databases and online broadcasts of proceedings.

- Fifty-State Legislative Tracking by Issue, *<www.ncsl.org/programs/ lis/lrl/50statetracking.htm>*, to search for legislative activity by issue and by state.

State Legislatures, State Laws, and State Regulations

- Website Links and Telephone Numbers, <*www.llsdc.org/state-leg/*>, from the Law Librarians Society of Washington, DC. A concise list of contact information for each state.

- The Thicket at State Legislatures, <*www.ncsl.typepad.com/the_ thicket/*>, a blog from the National Council of State Legislatures. The Thicket reports on state legislative news and links to other state political and legislative blogs.

§6.5 State Executive Branch Resources

Numerous professional organizations represent state executive branch officers. For governors, the largest organization is the National Governors Association. Other associations cover positions further down on the organization chart, such as the National Association of State Budget Officers, <*www.nasbo.org*>, and the National Association of State Energy Officials, <*www.naseo.org*>. The web sites for these organizations often provide valuable compilations of state information and policies on federal-state issues.

National Governors Association, <*www.nga.org*>, maintains several useful lists, including these two in the Governors Home section of the site:

- Governors' Contact Information.

- Governors' Staff Directories, including Washington representatives and policy directors.

The Council of State Governments, <*www.csg.org*>, a nonpartisan organization, reports on policy positions, legislation, interstate compacts, and trends in policy areas, such as Energy and Environment, in its State Trends & Policy section, <*www.csg.org/policy/*>.

The USA.gov web site has a brief section covering state-level associations and best practices resources at <*www.usa.gov/Government/State_ Local/News.shtml*>. State and Local Agencies and Offices, by Topic, <*www. usa.gov/Agencies/State_and_Territories/Agencies_by_Topic.shtml*>, a USA.gov list of links to, for example, all fifty state health agencies, all state elections offices, and all state corrections departments.

Governing.com, a commercial publication, provides a lengthy list of nationwide state professional associations at <*www.governing.com/gov links/glassn.htm*>.

§6.6 State Judicial Branch Resources

Each state has its own court system with its own court names and structure and its own approach to making information available. Web sites that make it easier to find information from and about the state courts are listed below.

- The National Center for State Courts, <*www.ncsconline.org*>, an independent and nonprofit organization, supports the courts with research and advocacy. Its web site provides information on court administration, data, and trends. The site's Information Services page, <*www.ncsconline.org/D_KIS/*>, includes links to state and local court web sites, state court structure charts, and the annual *Survey of Judicial Salaries*.

- The Law Library of Congress Guide to Law Online, <*www.loc.gov/ law/help/guide.php*>, maintains an extensive set of links to legal and judicial information from each state on its States & Territories page, <*www.loc.gov/law/help/guide/states.php*>.

- Legal Newsline, <*www.legalnewsline.com*>, reports news from the state supreme courts and attorneys general.

- Georgetown University Law Center: State Laws, <*www.ll.george town.edu/states/*>, contain web guides for doing legal research in each state or territory.

§6.10 International Government Internet Resources

§6.11 Web Directories

Several university web sites maintain lists of international government links.

- Foreign Government Links, from Northwestern University Libraries, <*www.library.northwestern.edu/govinfo/resource/ internat/foreign.html*>

- International Governmental Organizations (IGOs), <*www.library. northwestern.edu/govinfo/resource/internat/igo.html*>

- Nongovernmental Organizations (NGOs), from Duke University Libraries, *<http://library.duke.edu/research/subject/guides/ngo_guide/ngo_links/>*

§6.12 Country Information

The State Department, *<www.state.gov>* maintains a number of regular publications on its website providing information on countries, including:

- **Background Notes**, a classic and popular source for country profiles, updated regularly.

- **Diplomatic List**, a directory of diplomatic staff at foreign missions in the U.S.

- **Key Officers of Foreign Service Posts**, a list of top U.S. staff at U.S. missions abroad.

- **Independent States in the World and Dependencies and Areas of Special Sovereignty**, an official list of country names, indicating diplomatic relations status with the U.S.

The Central Intelligence Agency, *<www.cia.gov>*, also maintains several significant web publications on its site, including:

- **The World Factbook**, regularly updated national-level reference information on countries, territories, and dependencies.

- **World Leaders**, a regularly updated directory also known as **Chiefs of State and Cabinet Members of Foreign Governments**.

§6.13 World Legal Information

ASIL Electronic Resource Guides, *<www.asil.org/erghome.cfm>*, detail the research approaches and web resources on topics such as treaty research, international organizations research, the European Union, and the United Nations. ASIL is the American Society of International Law.

EISIL (Electronic Information System for International Law), *<www.eisil.org>*, maintained by the American Society of International Law, is an extensive database of official documents, web sites, and research guides related to international law.

Global and Comparative Law Resources, *<www.loc.gov/law/find/global.php>*, from the Library of Congress, provides legal news, documents, and research guides.

JURIST World Legal News, *<http://jurist.law.pitt.edu/worldlatest/>*, from the University of Pittsburgh Law School, provides current reporting on news related to international relations and agreements. The news reports link to the official documents (court opinions, treaties, transcripts) involved.

The State Department's publication, *Treaties in Force*, *<www.state. gov/s/l/treaty/treaties/>*, provides information on treaties and other international agreements to which the United States is a party. The Flare Index to Treaties web site, *<http://ials.sas.ac.uk/library/flag/introtreaties.htm>*, is a searchable database of basic information on over 1,500 significant multilateral (three or more parties) international treaties from 1856 to the present; the project was funded by the University of London.

§6.14 Global Search, News, and Statistics

Numerous organizations and individuals provide international information, news, and statistics on the web. Those listed below are a sample of useful sites.

- Search Engine Colossus, *<www.searchenginecolossus.com>*, has an extensive set of links to search engines and web directories around the world.

- World Newspapers and Magazines, *<www.world-newspapers.com>*, links to English-language online newspapers and news sites from around the globe.

- OECD.Stat Extracts, *<http://stats.oecd.org/WBOS/>*, provides numerous demographic, economic, and industry statistics from the Organisation for Economic Co-operation and Development, for OECD member countries.

- UNdata, *<http://data.un.org>*, serves as a portal to United Nations data collected from UN member states.

§6.99 Chapter Summary and Review Questions

Chapter Summary

Nongovernment web sites offer a variety of finding aids for U.S. state-level and international research. Use specialized search engines, directories, and guides to find information faster than with a general search engine.

Review Questions

- What web site could you use to find the web addresses for several state governments' web sites?
- The U.S. Conference of Mayors, *<www.usmayors.org>*, is the official nonpartisan organization of cities with populations of 30,000 or more. What type of information would you expect to find on its web site?
- Name two authoritative sources for finding basic information on countries.
- Where can you turn for assistance on international law topics?

Chapter Seven

Experts and Insiders

Often the best research resource is a person, rather than a web site, database, or book. This section includes basic information on finding experts and obtaining information via phone calls.

§7.0 Offline Resources: People

Not all information is online, and much of it is not recorded any-where but in the minds of experienced and knowledgeable people. Experts and insiders can be very helpful resources.

Your choice of phone or email may depend on how the source wishes to communicate. Email is convenient for people in other time zones, but can be limiting when you need to have an interactive conversation. Your interviews may also involve in-person meetings.

§7.1 When to Use People as an Information Source

✔ For information that has not been published online or in print.

✔ For opinions and insight into past, present, and future developments.

✔ For evaluative judgments about the information you have.

✔ For referrals to additional or better information sources.

✔ For a better understanding of how information and events are viewed by others.

§7.2 Preparing to Make an Information-Gathering Phone Call

✔ Make sure the answer is not readily available elsewhere.

✔ Do your homework. Try to get up to conversational level on a topic if you are calling an expert.

✔ Get background information on the person or organization you are calling to: a) confirm that this is an appropriate source and b) understand your source's role.

✔ Write down the questions you have or the information you need. Think about the best order in which to bring them up. While your conversation may not be a straight reading of questions, a list helps to ensure that you don't forget anything.

§7.3 Making the Call

✔ Introduce yourself by name and affiliation.

✔ Explain, concisely, why you are calling and how the information will be used ("I am writing a report for our membership and your work in this area is particularly important to us."). Let them know if you would like to quote them as a source, and get their permission to use their name, job title, and organization name in your research report.

✔ Listen to the response to be sure you have the proper person and that this is a good time to call.

✔ Ask your question, and then listen. Questions may be narrow ("Is this the correct title of the report?") or open-ended ("What do you think could happen next?").

✔ Don't worry when the conversation veers slightly off-topic. You may hear about facts or issues you had overlooked. At the very least, you will get a better understanding of what matters to your source.

✔ Don't hesitate to say that you are not sure you understand an issue. If necessary, restate what you think you understand and ask your contact if you have got it right.

✔ Wrap it up: Did you get all of the information you needed? Does the source have other sources to recommend? If necessary, can you make a follow-up call? What is the best time to call? Verify that you each have the other's phone number.

✔ Thank your contact, even if he or she has not been able to be helpful. If the source is important, you may wish to send a thank-you email or that rare species, the paper thank-you letter.

§7.10 Washington Contacts: Phone and Email

§7.11 Congress

Congressional staff can be useful sources of information on current congressional activities when that information is not available online, in print, or from other sources. Staff may be able to help you with future scheduling information or with very specific information on a bill they are currently handling.

Unfortunately, congressional staff phone directories are not available for free online. The Government Printing Office sells printed House and Senate telephone directories; see <*http://bookstore.gpo.gov*>. The Clerk of the House web site (<*http://clerk.house.gov*>) has House member and committee telephone directories, with links to Senate directories. However, the directories at the Clerk's site only provide the main office numbers; they do not list individual staff.

Several commercially published staff directories exist. For example, see the *Congressional Staff Directory* from Congressional Quarterly (*<http://csd.cq.com>*), the *Congressional Yellow Book* from Leadership Directories (*<www.leadershipdirectories.com>*), or the *Congressional Directory* (*<www.CongressionalDirectory.com>*) from TheCapitol.Net.

Congressional staff members are usually very busy; do your research first and use them only as a last resort.

§7.12 Executive Departments and Agencies

Staff members at federal agencies include experts in an incredible range of specialties in science, agriculture, industry, trade, demographics, and many other fields. Agencies also include program staff members who can assist you with grants, economic development, research sponsorship, and other opportunities.

The Federal Citizen Information Center, maintained by the U.S. General Services Administration, has a page of links to federal employee phone directories, by agency; see *<www.info.gov/phone.htm>*. Some online agency directories include email addresses.

Commercially published directories of federal staff include Leadership Directories' *Federal Yellow Book* (*<www.leadershipdirectories. com>*) and Carroll Publishing's Federal Directory and Federal Regional Directory, both listed at *<www.carrollpub.com>*.

§7.13 Media Contacts

Reporters for trade journals and those who cover a specific topic may be willing to share information, particularly if you have information to share with them. If you are working in a particular issue area, it is beneficial to know the names of the media covering that topic in Washington.

Hudson's Washington News Media Contacts Directory (*<www. greyhouse.com/hudsons.htm>*) lists news services and syndicates, specialized newsletters, radio and TV stations, columnists, freelance writers, and the reporters representing U.S. national and local papers and foreign news services in Washington. The *News Media Yellow Book* (*<www.leadershipdirectories.com>*) includes media contact information nationwide as well as many foreign media contacts.

§7.14 Selected Media Web Sites

This is a selective list from the *Congressional Deskbook*, § 13.51, and is on the web as a sample section from the *Deskbook* at *<CongressionalDeskbook.com>*.

Print Newspapers Online

- Washington Post, *<www.washingtonpost.com>*
- Washington Times, *<www.washtimes.com>*
- Christian Science Monitor, *<www.christianscience monitor.com>*
- Los Angeles Times, *<www.latimes.com>*
- New York Times, *<www.nytimes.com>*
- Wall Street Journal, *<www.wsj.com>*

Hill Newspapers

- Roll Call, *<www.rollcall.com>*
- The Hill, *<www.thehill.com>*

Legal Affairs

- Legal Times, *<www.legaltimes.com>*
- National Law Journal, *<www.nlj.com>*

Television

- ABC News, *<http://abcnews.go.com>*
- BBC News, *<http://news.bbc.co.uk>*
- C-SPAN, *<www.c-span.org>*
- CBS News, *<www.cbsnews.com>*
- CNN, *<www.cnn.com>*
- FOX News, *<www.foxnews.com>*
- NBC News, *<www.nbc.com/nbc/NBC_News/>*
- NewsHour with Jim Lehrer, *<www.pbs.org/newshour/>*

Radio

- C-SPAN Radio, *<www.c-span.org>*
- FederalNewsRadio.com, *<http://federalnewsradio.com>*
- National Public Radio, *<www.npr.org>*
- WTOP, *<www.wtopnews.com>*

On the Wires

- Associated Press, *<www.ap.org>*
- Reuters, *<www.reuters.com>*
- US Newswire, *<www.usnewswire.com/ topnews/current.htm>*
- Voice of America News, *<www.voanews.com>*

Weekly Magazines

- CQ Weekly, *<www.cq.com>*
- Economist, *<www.economist.com>*
- National Journal, *<http://nationaljournal.com>*
- Newsweek, *<www.newsweek.com>*
- Time, *<www.time.com/time/>*
- US News and World Report, *<www.usnews.com/usnews/ home.htm>*

Other

- National Press Club, *<http://npc.press.org>*

§7.15 Think Tanks

Washington think tanks or policy research institutes typically have an online directory of their subject experts, including email addresses, on their web sites. (For more information, see § 7.20, Think Tanks Online.)

§7.16 Trade and Professional Associations

Numerous national and international trade associations represent their members' interests in Washington. The larger associations have experts on industry and trade issues on staff. They can be a helpful source for legislative, regulatory, and other information specific to the association's concerns. The smaller associations may also be able to provide you with the information you need, or they may refer you to a contact elsewhere.

Among the larger industry associations that cover a wide range of issues are the United States Chamber of Commerce, <*www.uschamber.com*>; National Association of Manufacturers, <*www.nam.org*>; and National Federation of Independent Businesses, <*www.nfib.com*>. Major professional associations include the American Medical Association, <*www.ama-assn.org*>, and the National Education Association, <*www.nea.org*>. The Independent Sector, <*www.independentsector.org*>, represents nonprofit and philanthropic organizations.

Trade and professional association web sites usually do not include contact information for individual staff. Aside from a main number, they often provide email forms for submitting any inquiries not answered by the content on their web site.

Commercially published directories of associations include the *Association Yellow Book* from Leadership Directories, <*www.leadershipdirectories.com*>, and the *Encyclopedia of Associations* from Gale, <*www.gale.cengage.com*>. Columbia Books, <*www.columbiabooks.com*>, publishes both an association directory, <*www.associationexecs.com*>, and a lobbying firm directory, <*www.lobbyists.info*>.

§7.20 Think Tanks Online

"Think tank" is the popular name for a variety of organizations that conduct public policy research and education. Typically, they are nonprofit organizations. They may be independent or affiliated with a university, foundation, or other institution. They maintain staffs of specialized policy experts; they may also host visiting experts or contract with outside experts for research. Some cover a wide range of public policy issues, while others focus on a topic such as education, defense, or the federal budget. Many are associated with a specific ideology, such as limited government or the promotion of human rights.

Think-tank experts write reports and journal articles, give speeches and policy briefings, sit on discussion panels, and lead educational programs. Much of their work can be found on the think-tanks' web sites.

Resources commonly found on think-tank web sites include:

- Directories of their experts or staff subject expertise, with the experts' email addresses (sometimes found in the About Us section).
- A news/press/media center highlighting recent publications and statements on topical issues.
- Links to the text of their reports, briefings, and other releases organized by topic.
- An events section listing upcoming briefings and policy forums (often with the archived audio, video, or printed transcript for past events).
- An online book store, with policy books for purchase.

§7.21 Finding Think Tanks Online

The following sites provide directories of U.S. think tank web sites:

- FPRI Think Tank Directory, <*http://thinktanks.fpri.org/*>, from the Foreign Policy Research Institute, links to the web sites of U.S. think tanks focused on security and international affairs.

- World Think Tanks, <*www.policyjobs.net/World_Think_Tanks/*>, lists and describes think tanks from seven western nations, including the U.S. and Canada.

In addition, the National Journal Inc. sells a Washington directory called *The Capital Source* that includes a listing of Washington think tanks. Other sections in *The Capital Source* list contact information for Congress, the White House, the news media, trade associations, law and lobbying firms, and interest groups. For more information, see <*http://nationaljournal.com/about/capitalsource/*>.

The Global Go-To Guide to Think Tanks, <*www.sas.upenn.edu/irp/documents/2008_Global_Go_To_Think_Tanks.pdf*>, profiles the top think tanks in the U.S. and other countries. The study is by James G. McGann, Ph.D., of the University of Pennsylvania International Research Program.

§7.22 Selected Policy Institutes and Think Tanks

This is a selective list of think tanks online.

- American Enterprise Institute for Public Policy Research, *<www.aei.org>*
- Brookings Institution, *<www.brookings.org>*
- Carl Albert Congressional Research & Studies Center, *<www.ou.edu/special/albertctr/cachome.html>*
- Carnegie Endowment for International Peace, *<www.carnegieendowment.org>*
- Cato Institute, *<www.cato.org>*
- Center for a New American Security, *<www.cnas.org>*
- Center for American Progress, *<www.americanprogress.org>*
- Center for Congressional and Presidential Studies, *<http://spa.american.edu/ccps/>*
- Center for National Policy, *<www.cnponline.org>*
- Center for Strategic and International Studies, *<www.csis.org>*
- Center on Congress, *<http://congress.indiana.edu>*
- Center on Budget and Policy Priorities, *<www.cbpp.org>*
- Council on Foreign Relations, *<www.cfr.org>*
- Dirksen Congressional Center, *<www.dirksencongressionalcenter.org>*
- Heritage Foundation, *<www.heritage.org>*
- James A. Baker III Institute for Public Policy, *<http://bakerinstitute.org>*
- Joint Center for Political and Economic Studies, *<www.jointcenter.org>*
- National Bureau for Economic Research, *<www.nber.org>*
- National Center for Policy Analysis, *<www.ncpa.org>*
- New America Foundation, *<www.newamerica.net>*
- Peterson Institute for International Economics, *<www.iie.com>*
- Progressive Policy Institute, *<www.ppionline.org>*
- The Public Forum Institute, *<www.publicforuminstitute.org>*
- RAND Corporation, *<www.rand.org>*
- Urban Institute, *<www.urban.org>*
- Woodrow Wilson International Center for Scholars, *<www.wilsoncenter.org>*

§7.99 Chapter Summary and Review Questions

Chapter Summary

Critical information and insight that cannot be found on the web or in print resides in the minds of experienced experts and insiders. Learn how to find experts, when to stop searching and pick up the phone, and how to approach an information-gathering phone call.

Review Questions

- When might you want to talk to an expert or insider rather than searching for information online?
- When making a research phone call, what information should you provide at the start of the call?
- What is a think tank and what type of information can you typically find on a think-tank web site?

Table of Web Sites

References are to chapter and section numbers.

Name	URL	Section
ABC News	http://abcnews.go.com	7.14
Administrative Office of the U.S. Courts	www.uscourts.gov	4.30
AllPlus	www.allplus.com	2.1
Allwhois	http://allwhois.com	2.44
AltLaw	http://altlaw.org	4.30
American Enterprise Institute for Public Policy Research	www.aei.org	7.22
American FactFinder	http://factfinder.census.gov	6.2
American Medical Association	www.ama-assn.org	7.16
American Presidency Project	www.presidency.ucsb.edu	5.22
Appropriations Fiscal Year 2009	http://thomas.loc.gov/home/approp/app09.html	3.40
ASIL (American Society of International Law) Electronic Resource Guides	www.asil.org/erghome.cfm	6.13
Ask.com	www.ask.com	2.1
Associated Press	www.ap.org	7.14
Association Yellow Book	www.leadership directories.com	7.16
BBC News	http://news.bbc.co.uk	7.14
beSpacific	www.bespacific.com	2.53
Best of the Business Web	www.jjhill.org/research_online/best_of_the_business_web.cfm	2.11
Bing	www.bing.com	2.1
The Bluebook: A Uniform System of Citation, 18th edition	www.legalbluebook.com	1.4, 4.30
Brookings Institution	www.brookings.org	7.22
Capitol Source	http://nationaljournal.com/about/capitalsource	7.21
Carl Albert Congressional Research & Studies Center	www.ou.edu/special/albertctr/cachome.html	7.22

Name	URL	Section
Carnegie Endowment for International Peace	www.carnegieendowment.org	7.22
Carroll Publishing	www.carrollpub.com	7.12
Cato Institute	www.cato.org	7.22
CBS News	www.cbsnews.com	7.14
CENDI.gov	www.cendi.gov	1.3
Center for American Progress	www.americanprogress.org	7.22
Center for a New American Security	www.cnas.org	7.22
Center for Congressional and Presidential Studies	http://spa.american.edu/ccps	7.22
Center for Democracy & Technology	www.cdt.org	3.80
Center for National Policy	www.cnponline.org	7.22
Center for Strategic and International Studies	www.csis.org	7.22
Center on Budget and Policy Priorities	www.cbpp.org	7.22
Center on Congress	http://congress.indiana.edu	7.22
Chicago Manual of Style	www.chicagomanualofstyle.org	1.4
Christian Science Monitor	www.christiansciencemonitor.com	7.14
CIA (Central Intelligence Agency)	www.cia.gov	6.12
Clerk of the House	http://clerk.house.gov	3.14, 7.11
	www.house.gov	Ch. 3
CNN	www.cnn.com	7.14
Code of Federal Regulations	www.archives.gov/federal-register/tutorial/index.html	5.41
	www.fdsys.gov	5.45
	www.gpoaccess.gov/cfr	5.44
Columbia Books	www.columbiabooks.com	7.16
Congressional Bills: Glossary	www.gpoaccess.gov/bills/glossary.html	3.15
Congressional Budget Office (CBO)	www.cbo.gov/listserver	3.50

Name	URL	Section
Congressional Deskbook	**CongressionalDeskbook.com**	3.41, 3.43, 7.14
Congressional Directory	**www.Congressional Directory.com**	7.11
Congressional Record	**http://thomas.loc.gov/ home/rss/dd.xml**	3.50
Congressional Research Service (CRS)	**www.loc.gov/crsinfo**	3.80
Congressional Staff Directory	**http://csd.cq.com**	7.11
Congressional Yellow Book	**www.leadership directories.com**	7.11
Consumer Product Safety Commission	**www.cpsc.gov/cpscpub/ prerel/rss.html**	2.55
Copyright Clearance Center, Inc.	**www.copyright.com**	1.3
Cornell University Legal Information Institute	**www.law.cornell.edu/ citation/index.htm**	4.40
	www.law.cornell.edu/supct	4.20, 5.10
	www.law.cornell.edu/uscode	3.60
Council of State Governments	**www.csg.org/policy**	6.5
Council on Foreign Relations	**www.cfr.org**	7.22
CQ.com	**www.cq.com**	2.56, 3.50
CQ Press	**www.cqpress.com**	2.12
CQ Weekly	**www.cq.com**	7.14
Creative Commons	**http://creativecommons.org**	1.3
C-SPAN	**www.c-span.org**	7.14
C-SPAN Radio	**www.c-span.org**	7.14
Delicious	**http://delicious.com**	2.11
Department of Defense (DOD)	**www.defenselink.mil/ news/rss**	2.55
Diigo	**www.diigo.com**	1.4
Dirksen Congressional Center	**www.dirksen congressionalcenter.org**	7.22
DocuTicker	**www.docuticker.com**	2.53
DomainTools Whois	**www.domaintools.com**	2.44
Dow Jones Factiva	**www.factiva.com**	2.56

Name	URL	Section
DTIC Online	www.dtic.mil	5.12
Duke University Libraries	http://library.duke.edu/research/subject/guides/ngo_guide/ngo_links	6.11
Economist	www.economist.com	7.14
e-Government and Web Directory: U.S. Federal Government, Online	www.bernanpress.com	2.12
EISIL (Electronic Information System for International Law)	www.eisil.org	6.13
Encyclopedia of Associations	www.gale.cengage.com	7.16
Environmental Protection Agency (EPA)—Federal Register Environmental Documents	www.epa.gov/fedrgstr	5.48
Evernote	http://evernote.com	1.4
Executive Order disposition tables	www.archives.gov/federalregister/executive-orders/disposition.html	5.21
FactCheck.org	www.factcheck.org	2.42
FCC Radio and Television Station Filings	http://svartifoss2.fcc.gov/prod/cdbs/pubacc/prod/cdbs_pa.htm	5.60
FDsys	www.fdsys.gov	3.21, 5.23, 5.24, 5.43, 5.45
FEC Campaign Filings Report	www.fec.gov/disclosure.shtml	5.60
Federal Citizen Information Center	www.info.gov/phone.htm	7.12
Federal Directory	www.carrollpub.com	7.12
Federal Judicial Center	www.fjc.gov	4.30
Federal Judicial Opinions	http://pacer.psc.uscourts.gov	4.30
	www.law.cornell.edu/federal/opinions.html	4.30
Federal Judicial Vacancies	www.uscourts.gov/judicialvac.html	4.30
Federal Legislative History Documents	www.llsdc.org/elec-leghist-docs	3.20
FederalNewsRadio.com	http://federalnewsradio.com	7.14

Name	URL	Section
Federal Register	http://listserv.access.gpo.gov	2.51
	www.archives.gov/federal-register/cfr/about.html	5.46
	www.archives.gov/federal-register/tutorial/index.html	5.41
	www.fdsys.gov/fdsys/browse/collection.action?collectionCode=FR	5.41, 5.43
	www.federalregister.gov/inspection.aspx	5.41
Federal Yellow Book	www.leadershipdirectories.com	7.12
Federation of American Scientists (FAS)	www.fas.org/irp/offdocs/direct.htm	5.22
	www.fas.org/sgp/crs	3.80
FedStats.gov	www.fedstats.gov	6.2
FindLaw	http://dictionary.lp.findlaw.com	4.50
	www.findlaw.com	2.11, Ch. 4, 4.20, 5.10
Flare Index to Treaties	http://ials.sas.ac.uk/library/flag/introtreaties.htm	6.13
FOX News	www.foxnews.com	7.14
FPRI Think Tank Directory	http://thinktanks.fpri.org	7.21
Freedom of Information Act	www.gwu.edu/nsarchiv/nsa/foia	5.51
	www.justice.gov/04foia/foiacontacts.htm	5.51
	www.pueblo.gsa.gov/cic_text/fed_prog/foia/foia.htm	5.51
	www.usdoj.gov/04foia/04_7.html	5.51
GalleryWatch	www.gallerywatch.com	2.56, 3.50, 3.80
General Services Administration (GSA)	www.pueblo.gsa.gov/cic_text/fed_prog/foia/foia.htm	5.51
	www.reginfo.gov	5.48

Name	URL	Section
Georgetown University Law Library	www.ll.george town.edu/find	2.11
	www.ll.georgetown.edu/ guides/freelowcost.cfm	4.31
	www.ll.georgetown.edu/ guides/presidential_ documents.cfm	5.22
	www.ll.georgetown.edu/ research	4.30
	www.ll.georgetown.edu/ states	6.6
	www.ll.georgetown.edu/ tutorials/admin/index.html	5.48
Global and Comparative Law Resources	www.loc.gov/law/find/ global.php	6.13
globalEDGE	http://globaledge.msu.edu	2.11
Global Go-To Guide to Think Tanks	www.sas.upenn.edu/irp/ documents/2008_Global_ Go_To_Think_Tanks.pdf	7.21
Google	http://reader.google.com	2.54
	www.google.com	2.1
	www.google.com/help/ cheatsheet.html	2.32
	www.google.com/unclesam	5.12
Governing.com	www.governing.com/ govlinks/glassn.htm	6.5
Government Accountability Office (GAO)	www.gao.gov/subscribe	2.51, 3.50
GovTrack.us	www.govtrack.com	3.50
GPO Access	www.gpoaccess.gov	2.30, Ch. 3, 3.20
	www.gpoaccess.gov/ bills/glossary.html	3.15
	www.gpoaccess.gov/ executive.html	5.21
	www.gpoaccess.gov/uscode	3.60

Name	URL	Section
GPO FDsys	**www.fdsys.gov**	2.30, Ch. 3, 5.21
GPO Federal Depository Library Directory	**www.gpoaccess.gov/ libraries.html**	3.60
GPO Federal Depository Library Program	**www.gpo.gov/libraries**	3.21
GPO House and Senate telephone directories	**http://bookstore.gpo.gov**	7.11
GPO Online Bookstore	**http://bookstore.gpo.gov**	3.60
Harvard Business School Citation Guide	**www.library.hbs.edu/guides/ citationguide.pdf**	1.4
Heritage Foundation	**www.heritage.org**	7.22
Hill, The	**www.thehill.com**	7.14
House Law Revision Counsel	**http://uscode.house.gov**	3.60, 3.70
House Lobby Reports	**http://lobbying disclosure.house.gov**	3.82
House Majority Whip	**http://majoritywhip. house.gov/daily_whipline**	3.50
House Republican Whip	**http://republicanwhip. house.gov**	3.50
House Rules Committee	**http://rules.house.gov**	3.50
Hudson's Washington News Media Contacts Directory	**www.greyhouse.com/ hudsons.htm**	7.13
Independent Sector, The	**www.independentsector.org**	7.16
InfoPeople Search Engine Guides	**http://infopeople.org/ search/chart.html**	2.3
	http://infopeople.org/ search/tools.html	2.3
Institute for Research on Poverty	**www.irp.wisc.edu**	1.1
Internet Public Library (IPL)	**www.ipl.org**	2.11
Intute	**www.intute.ac.uk**	2.11
James A. Baker III Institute for Public Policy	**http://bakerinstitute.org**	7.22
Joint Center for Political and Economic Studies	**www.jointcenter.org**	7.22
Judges of the U.S. Courts	**www.fjc.gov/history/home.nsf**	4.30

Name	URL	Section
JURIST World Legal News	http://jurist.law.pitt.edu/ worldlatest	6.13
Justia	http://law.justia.com/us	4.30
Law Librarians' Society of Washington, DC	www.llsdc.org	3.20
Law Library of Congress	www.loc.gov/law/find/ global.php	6.13
	www.loc.gov/law/help/ guide.php	6.6
	www.loc.gov/law/help/ guide/states.php	6.6
Leadership Directories	www.leadership directories.com	7.11
Legal Information Institute	www.law.cornell.edu	4.20
Legal Newsline	www.legalnewsline.com	6.6
Legal Reference and Research Tools	www.thecapitol.net/ Research/legalFTL.htm	Ch. 4
Legal Times	www.legaltimes.com	7.14
LexisNexis	www.lexisnexis.com	2.56, 3.50, Ch. 4
Library of Congress	http://catalog.loc.gov	2.20
List of CFR Sections Affected	www.gpoaccess.gov/lsa	5.44
Lobbyists	www.lobbyists.info	7.16
	www.senate.gov/lobby	3.82
Loislaw.com	Loislaw.com	Ch. 4
Los Angeles Times	www.latimes.com	7.14
Map-Stats	www.fedstats.gov/qf	6.2
Media Relations Handbook	MediaRelationsHandbook.com	5.51
National Agricultural Law Center	www.nationalaglaw center.org/crs	3.80
National Archives and Record Administration	www.archives.gov	5.21, 5.46
National Association of Manufacturers	www.nam.org	7.16
National Association of Secretaries of State	www.nass.org	6.0

Name	URL	Section
National Association of State Budget Officers	www.nasbo.org	6.5
National Association of State Energy Officials	www.naseo.org	6.5
National Bureau for Economic Research	www.nber.org	7.22
National Center for Policy Analysis	www.ncpa.org	7.22
National Center for State Courts	www.ncsconline.org	6.6
National Council of State Legislatures	www.ncsl.org	6.4
National Education Association	www.nea.org	7.16
National Federation of Independent Businesses	www.nfib.com	7.16
National Governors Association	www.nga.org	6.0, 6.5
National Journal	http://nationaljournal.com	7.14
National Law Journal	www.nlj.com	7.14
National Press Club	http://npc.press.org	7.14
National Public Radio	www.npr.org	7.14
National Security Archive	www.gwu.edu/~nsarchiv	5.50
National Trade and Professional Associations of the U.S.	www.associationexecs.com	7.16
NBC News	www.nbc.com/nbc/ NBC_News	7.14
New America Foundation	www.newamerica.net	7.22
Newsgator Technologies	www.newsgator.com	2.54
NewsHour with Jim Lehrer	www.pbs.org/newshour	7.14
News Media Yellow Book	www.leadership directories.com	7.13
Newsweek	www.newsweek.com	7.14
New York Times	www.nytimes.com	7.14
Nolo's Legal Glossary	www.nolo.com/glossary.cfm	4.50
Nongovernmental Organizations (NGOs)	http://library.duke.edu/ research/subject/guides/ ngo_guide/ngo_links	6.11

Name	URL	Section
Northwestern University Libraries: Foreign Governments	**www.library.northwestern. edu/govinfo/resource/ internat/foreign.html**	6.11
Northwestern University Libraries: International Governmental Organizations	**www.library.northwestern. edu/govinfo/resource/ internat/igo.html**	6.11
Office of Information and Regulatory Affairs (OIRA)	**www.reginfo.gov**	5.48
	www.whitehouse.gov/ omb/inforeg_regmatters	5.48
Office of Management and Budget (OMB)	**www.whitehouse.gov/omb**	5.23, 5.24
OMB Watch	**www.ombwatch.org/ regresources**	5.48
OpenCongress	**www.opencongress.org**	3.50
Open CRS	**http://opencrs.com**	3.80
Opensecrets.org	**www.opensecrets.org**	5.60
Organisation for Economic Co-operation and Development (OECD)	**http://stats.oecd.org/WBOS**	6.14
PACER (Public Access to Court Electronic Records)	**http://pacer.psc.uscourts.gov**	4.30
Pandia Search Central	**www.pandia.com**	2.38
Peterson Institute for International Economics	**www.iie.com**	7.22
PolitiFact	**www.politifact.com**	2.42
Presidential Documents	**www.archives.gov/ presidential-libraries/ research/guide.html**	5.21
Presidential Libraries	**www.archives.gov/ presidential-libraries**	5.21
President's Budget Documents		
GPO FDsys	**www.fdsys.gov**	5.23
Office of Management and Budget	**www.whitehouse.gov/omb**	5.23
Progressive Policy Institute	**www.ppionline.org**	7.22
Public Forum Institute	**www.publicforuminstitute.org**	7.22

Name	URL	Section
Public Laws Electronic Notification Service	www.archives.gov/federal-register/laws/updates.html	2.51
Public Library of Law	www.plol.org	4.30
RAND Corporation	www.rand.org	7.22
RegInfo	www.reginfo.gov	5.48
Regulations.gov	www.regulations.gov	5.48
Republican Cloakroom	http://repcloakroom.house.gov	3.50
Resources for Documenting Sources in the Disciplines	http://owl.english.purdue.edu/owl/resource/ 585/02	1.4
Resource Shelf	www.resourceshelf.com	2.38
Reuters	www.reuters.com	7.14
Roll Call	www.rollcall.com	7.14
SCOTUSblog	www.scotusblog.com	2.53
Search Engine Colossus	www.searchenginecolossus.com	6.14
SEC IDEA	www.sec.gov/idea/searchidea/webusers.htm	5.60
Securities and Exchange Commission (SEC)	www.secinfo.com	5.60
Senate, U.S.	www.senate.gov	Ch. 3
Senate Lobby Reports	www.senate.gov/lobby	3.82
Small Business Administration Regulatory Alerts	www.sba.gov/advo/laws/law_regalerts.html	5.48
Snopes.com	www.snopes.com	2.42
Soople	www.soople.com	2.1
State Agency Databases	http://wikis.ala.org/godort/index.php/State_Agency_Databases	6.1
State Capital Newspapers	www.ncsl.org/programs/press/dailynews/cpapers.htm	6.2
State Courts	www.ncsconline.org	6.6
State Department, U.S.	www.state.gov	6.12
State Department Foreign Press Center	http://fpc.state.gov/c18185.htm	3.80

Name	URL	Section
State Legislatures, State Laws, and State Regulations	www.llsdc.org/state-leg.htm	6.4
Stateline.org	www.stateline.org	6.2
State of the Union Addresses	www.presidency.ucsb.edu	5.22
Statutes at Large		
GPO	www.gpoaccess.gov/statutes	3.60
GPO Federal Depository Library Directory	www.gpoaccess.gov/libraries.html	3.60
GPO Online Bookstore	http://bookstore.gpo.gov	3.60
Supreme Court Opinions		
FindLaw	http://supreme.lp.findlaw.com/supreme_court/resources.html	4.20
	www.findlaw.com/casecode/supreme.html	4.20
Legal Information Institute	www.law.cornell.edu/supct	4.20
U.S. Supreme Court	www.supremecourtus.gov	4.0, 4.20
TheCapitol.Net	www.thecapitol.net	3.15, Ch. 4
Congressional and Legislative Terms	www.thecapitol.net/glossary	3.15
Congressional Deskbook	CongressionalDeskbook.com	3.41
Congressional Directory	www.CongressionalDirectory.com	7.11
Congressional Documents	congressional documents.com	3.15
Federal Regulatory Process Poster	www.RegulatoryProcess.com	5.48
Legal Reference and Research Tools	www.thecapitol.net/Research/legalFTL.htm	Ch. 4
	www.thecapitol.net/Publications/agencyposter.htm	5.40
THOMAS	http://thomas.loc.gov	2.20, 3.20, 3.30
Time	www.time.com/time	7.14
Treaties in Force	www.state.gov/s/l/treaty/treaties	6.13

Name	URL	Section
Ubernote	www.ubernote.com	1.4
United Nations	http://data.un.org	6.14
University of California at Berkeley	www.lib.berkeley.edu/TeachingLib/Guides/Internet/FindInfo.html	2.38
University of Maryland School of Law	www.law.umaryland.edu/marshall/crsreports	3.80
University of Michigan Documents Center	www.lib.umich.edu/govdocs	2.11
University of Pittsburgh Law School	http://jurist.law.pitt.edu/worldlatest	6.13
University of Virginia Library	http://www2.lib.virginia.edu	4.0
	www.lib.virginia.edu/govdocs/fed_decisions_agency.html	5.48
Urban Institute	www.urban.org	7.22
U.S. Chamber of Commerce	www.uschamber.com	7.16
U.S. Code		
GPO Access	www.gpoaccess.gov/uscode	3.70
House Law Revision Counsel	http://uscode.house.gov	3.70
Legal Information Institute	www.law.cornell.edu/uscode	3.70
U.S. Conference of Mayors	www.usmayors.org	6.99
U.S. Congress	http://thomas.loc.gov	Ch. 3
U.S. Copyright Office	www.copyright.gov	1.3
U.S. Court of Appeals for Veterans Claims	www.vetapp.gov	4.0
U.S. Court of Federal Claims	www.uscfc.uscourts.gov	4.0
U.S. Court of International Trade	www.cit.uscourts.gov	4.0
U.S. Courts Administrative Office	www.uscourts.gov	4.30
U.S. Courts of Appeal	www.uscourts.gov/courtlinks	4.0
U.S. District Courts	www.uscourts.gov/courtlinks	4.0
U.S. Federal Circuit Courts	www.uscourts.gov/courtlinks	4.10
U.S. government	ChildStats.gov.	5.10
	EconomicIndicators.gov	5.10
	FedStats.gov	5.10

Name	URL	Section
	http://usasearch.gov	5.12, 6.1
	www.usa.gov	Ch. 5, 5.10
U.S. Government Manual, 2008-2009	www.gpoaccess.gov/ gmanual	5.0
U.S. House of Representatives	www.house.gov	Ch. 3
US News and World Report	www.usnews.com/ usnews/home.htm	7.14
US Newswire	www.usnewswire.com/ topnews/current.htm	7.14
U.S. Senate	www.senate.gov	Ch. 3
U.S. State Department	www.state.gov	6.12
U.S. Supreme Court	www.supremecourtus.gov	4.0, 4.20
U.S. Tax Court	www.ustaxcourt.gov	4.0
USA.gov	www.usa.gov	2.11, 2.51, 2.55, 6.3, 6.5
USAsearch.gov	www.usasearch.gov	5.12, 6.1
USDA Food Safety & Inspection Service	www.fsis.usda.gov/regulations	5.48
Versuslaw.com	Versuslaw.com	Ch. 4
Voice of America News	www.voanews.com	7.14
Wall Street Journal	www.wsj.com	2.53, 7.14
Washington Information Directory	www.cqpress.com	2.12
Washington Post	www.washingtonpost.com	7.14
Washington Times	www.washtimes.com	7.14
Washington Wire	http://blogs.wsj.com/ washwire	2.53
Westlaw	http://west.thomson.com	2.56, 3.50, 3.60, Ch. 4
White House	www.whitehouse.gov	5.21
Whois Source	http://allwhois.com	2.44
Woodrow Wilson International Center for Scholars	www.wilsoncenter.org	7.22

Name	URL	Section
World Newspapers and Magazines	**www.world-newspapers.com**	6.14
World Think Tanks	**www.policyjobs.net/ World_Think_Tanks**	7.21
WTOP	**www.wtopnews.com**	7.14
Yahoo! Help	**http://help.yahoo.com/ l/us/yahoo/search**	2.32
Yahoo! News	**http://news.yahoo.com/rss**	2.55
Yahoo! Search	**http://search.yahoo.com**	2.1
Zotero	**www.zotero.org**	1.4

Index

References are to chapter and section numbers.

About TheCapitol.Net

We help you understand how Washington and Congress work.™

*TheCapitol.Net is a non-partisan business that came out of
Congressional Quarterly, (CQ) in 1999. CQ had offered many
of the same courses and workshops since the 1970s.*

*Instruction includes topics on the legislative and budget process, congressional
operations, public and foreign policy development, advocacy and media training,
business etiquette and writing. All training includes course materials.*

*TheCapitol.Net encompasses a dynamic team of more than 150 faculty members
and authors, all of whom are independent subject matter experts and veterans in
their fields. Faculty and authors include senior government executives, former
Members of Congress, Hill and agency staff, editors and journalists,
lobbyists, lawyers, nonprofit executives and scholars.*

*All courses, seminars and workshops can be tailored to align with your
organization's educational objectives and presented on-site at your location.
We've worked with hundreds of clients across the country to develop
and produce a wide variety of custom, on-site training.*

Our practitioner books and publications are written by leading subject matter experts.

*TheCapitol.Net has more than 2,000 clients representing
congressional offices, federal and state agencies, military branches,
corporations, associations, news media and NGOs nationwide.*

Our blog: Hobnob Blog—hit or miss ... give or take ... this or that ...

TheCapitol.Net is on Yelp.

**TheCapitol.Net supports the
TC Williams Debate Society, Wikimedia Foundation
and the Sunlight Foundation**

TheCapitol.Net

Non-partisan training and publications that show how Washington works.™

PO Box 25706, Alexandria, VA 22313-5706   703-739-3790   www.TheCapitol.Net

CPSIA information can be obtained at www.ICGtesting.com
Printed in the USA
LVOW071728250112

265550LV00002B/5/P